THE
STORY
OF
TAYTO

The Original Irish Crisp

BOBBY AHERNE

It is impossible to thank every person who has contributed to the Tayto story over the past 70 years, but the author and Tayto would like to offer thanks to the following people for their generosity of time, knowledge and energy in the creation of this book: Barry Murphy, Yvonne Brady, Peter Murphy, Stephen Murphy, Anthony Donnelly, Charles Coyle, John O'Connor, Fionnuala Ryan, Louise Myler, Terry Myler, Maïa Dunphy, Paula Kelly, Anne Darbey, Nick McGivney, Myles McWeeney, Pearse McCaughey, Gerry Byrne, Tom McInerney, Frances Sweeney, Carol McCaghy and Alina Uí Chaollaí. Special thanks to Karla Devenney for her tireless work researching the Tayto press and photographic archives, and to all the Tayto staff down through the years who have played their part in this very Irish story.

First published 2024 by Sitric Books,
An imprint of The Lilliput Press Ltd.
62–63 Sitric Road,
Arbour Hill,
Dublin 7,
Ireland
www.lilliputpress.ie

10 9 8 7 6 5 4 3 2 1

A CIP record for this title is available from The British Library.

ISBN 978-1-84351-913-3

Design and typesetting by Sarah McCoy
Set in 11pt on 15pt Futura PT
Printed and bound in Czechia by Finidr

CONTENTS

The Tayto logo through the ages.

INTRODUCTION: A TIME BEFORE TAYTO

For many years now, people have been debating the correct term for thin slices of potatoes, cooked until crunchy. Americans call them 'potato chips'; the English call them 'crisps'. The Irish tend to sit this argument out, because we have our very own special word for the delicacy. For the past seventy years, we've been calling them 'Taytos' (or indeed, sometimes, 'a package o' crips').

But where did Taytos come from? How has Tayto managed to infiltrate every warm childhood memory centred around a school tour, tuck shop, packed lunch, birthday party, day trip, picnic, visit to the newsagents and every neglected afternoon spent in the corner of a pub – as well as many more adult memories besides? How did Tayto become so inextricably linked to Irishness in such a relatively short period of time? Why is Tayto always the number one foodstuff that emigrants miss about Ireland? In a country that doesn't have a particularly vast cuisine, does the Tayto sandwich – consisting of Tayto crisps, soft Irish bread and creamy Irish butter – represent the zenith of our culinary accomplishments? Do flavoured crisps really belong on a list – alongside cream crackers, ejection seats, Milk of Magnesia, induction coils, hypodermic syringes and the modern submarine – of ingenious Irish innovations? To the latter question, the short answer is 'yes'. The *long* answer to all of these questions, however, tells a story about more than just a crisp. It's a story about Irish industry, culture, society and advertising – and, of course, food – over the last seven decades.

It begins, as all good stories should, around 8,000 years ago, on the shores of Lake Titicaca – when the potato was first domesticated from a wild species native to the Andes. Thousands of years later, after the Spanish conquest of the Inca Empire, spuds eventually ended up back in Europe and were introduced to Cork by Spaniards in the 1580s. Within a couple of hundred years, two million acres across Ireland were dedicated to growing

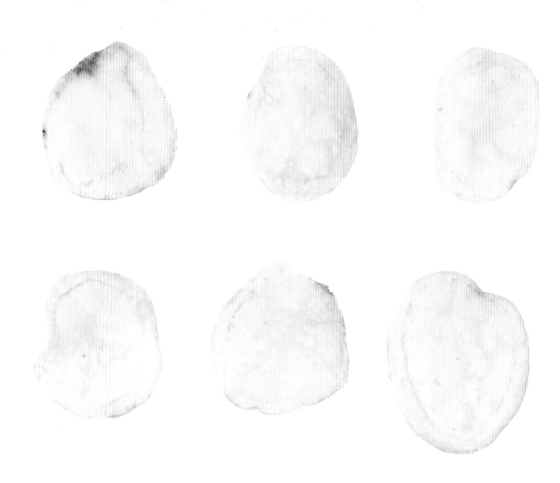

potatoes and the Irish diet was 90 per cent potato-based. Our whirlwind love affair with the humble spud – or at least with the boiled, mashed and roasted varieties – had begun in earnest. And they weren't even crunchy yet!

In 1817, one of the world's first celebrity chefs, William Kitchiner, published a bestselling cookbook called *The Cook's Oracle*. Recipe number 104 sees the Londoner instructing readers to cut potatoes 'as you would peel a lemon', then fry the pieces in lard 'till they are crisp', and 'send them up with a very little salt sprinkled over them.' At the time, he christened this dish 'Potatoes fried in Slices or Shavings' – but it's what we would now call 'Ready Salted Crisps'. Some time later, Granite State Potato Chip Factory – opened in New Hampshire, USA, in 1905 – became

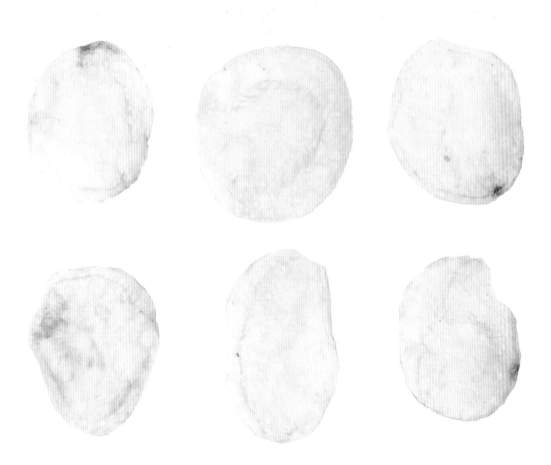

one of the first commercial 'potato chip' companies in the world, selling plain crisps in paper bags. The following decade, Smith's Potato Crisp Company was founded in London, with Frank Smith later pioneering the concept of a small blue sachet of salt in each bag. Smith's crisps were available in Ireland until the Anglo-Irish Trade War of the 1930s, when harsh tariffs were imposed on imports from Britain. In the 40s, a few short-lived Irish crisp companies popped up, including Johnny Sheehan's in Arklow and Star Crisps in Cork and Clontarf. But here in Ireland, and across the world, crisps still lacked a certain... *je ne sais quoi.*

But then ... along came a Dubliner by the name of Joseph Murphy ...

THE
FOUNDING
FATHER

A young Joe Murphy, with his brother Jack and sister Patricia –
both of whom would later help out at Joe's businesses over the years.

A LIBERTIES CHILDHOOD

On Tuesday the 15th of May 1923, just five months after the foundation of the Irish Free State, Dubliner Molly Sweeney and Kilkenny native Thomas Murphy welcomed their fifth child into the world – a fair-haired, blue-eyed baby boy named Joseph Mary Murphy.

The Murphys lived at 149 Thomas Street in Dublin, in the heart of The Liberties and in the shadow of the Guinness brewery just across the road. Molly had a wallpaper and paint shop on the ground floor of the house, while Thomas – one of the city's leading suppliers of timber scaffolding – ran a builders' providers from the yard at the back. A couple of doors up from them was The Irish Agricultural and Wholesale Society. Decades later, the site of the Murphy home (and seven others on that block) would be cleared to make way for a car park. The legacy of that house, however, would live on, through the hardy business acumen that it fostered in its residents.

Growing up with this duality of retail and craftsmanship literally on his doorstep made its mark on Joe, whose entrepreneurial eye was first stirred by some leftover bits of scrap wood in his father's yard. Rather than let the wood go to waste, he realized that there was some extra pocket money to be made by chopping it up, throwing it into a wheelbarrow, and selling it as kindling in the bustling marketplace that was Thomas Street at the time. He and his friends would also collect stray glass bottles, returning them to redeem the deposit on them.

A keen young cyclist, Joe's most treasured possession was his 'Fairy' bike with a cargo compartment on the back, which he could use to transport his wares. By his early teenage years, Joe was sending off some of his firewood earnings to the USA in exchange for a different type of wood product: comic books. To help him with his dyslexia, Joe's mother had bought him a few comic books, hoping that they would provide a gateway towards reading. And they were. As an adult, Joe would voraciously read every newspaper and trade magazine from cover to cover, and would cover every book in his library with scrawled notes in the margins. But the comics were also a gateway to *another* money-making scheme: by purchasing comics that weren't available in Ireland, he was acquiring a rare commodity, much sought-after by his peers. After waiting months for a new batch to arrive by steamship, he'd read them and then rent out individual issues to his friends and friends of friends. This lending library was a mutually beneficial arrangement. Not only would Joe make his money back, but the other kids also got to enjoy the latest funnies and serials from across the pond at a fraction of their cover price.

It wouldn't be long before Joe was putting all of his experience, research and learnings to good use.

It is perhaps unsurprising that Joe would *also* be an early adopter of Dale Carnegie's 1936 book *How to Win Friends and Influence People* – a book that he would gift to his children, decades later. A formative publication in the self-help genre, Carnegie's multi-million-selling tome purports to teach its reader about leadership skills, methods of effective communication, and making ideas happen. It wouldn't be long before Joe was putting all of his experience, research and learnings to good use.

Around the time that the Second World War kicked off on the Continent, Joe abandoned his studies at Synge Street CBS – an inner-city school that would produce many leading figures of 20th-century Ireland, from Flann O'Brien and Gay Byrne to a taoiseach and a president – in pursuit of a career. He was already a couple of years beyond the official school leaving age of the era (fourteen), likely due to the relative financial comfort of being from a small family that had been reduced, tragically, from

(ABOVE) Back row: Tommy (Joe's father) and Joe. Front row: Patricia, Jack and Jack's wife Maureen.

(BELOW) Joe in London, encountering some of the local wildlife.

seven members to five. Joe's eldest brother, Tommy, had entered the priesthood, but contracted tuberculosis in Rome during the epidemic of the 30s. He showed no improvement during a stay at the Great St Bernard Hospice in Switzerland, so he returned home to Thomas Street, where the attic was turned into an isolation room for him. Unfortunately, his brother Patrick snuck up to visit his lonely brother and also ended up contracting the disease. Tommy passed away in 1934, followed by Paddy three years later. As a result of this, Joe found himself being mollycoddled and spoiled by his parents. This, however, didn't prevent him from putting on the poor mouth to his own kids, decades later, to emphasize how easy they had it. 'When I was your age, we were so poor that I didn't even have shoes,' his son Barry recalls him saying – before being interrupted by his fact-checking sister Patricia. 'That's not true, Joe,' she replied. 'You had the best shoes!'

HUMBLE BEGINNINGS

Thankfully, Joe didn't find himself drawn to the ecclesiastical lifestyle. 'To hell with this,' he allegedly declared. 'We need one sinner in the family!' After school, a timepiece-loving Joe spent a couple of years in Waterford, serving an apprenticeship to a clock-maker. In a letter to his mother, he complained about the cold linoleum flooring of the shop's living quarters – so Molly sent him back a couple of rugs. In the meantime, his sole surviving brother Jack followed their father into the building trade – and was always on hand to fix any structural issues with Tayto's factories over the years.

Upon Joe's return to Dublin, he took a job in the storeroom of James J. Fox, a renowned cigar and whiskey emporium directly opposite Trinity College. Joe soon progressed to sales, working behind the counter of the shop. It was here that he learned about the importance of creating an enchanting atmosphere, and the power of alluring scents. Within a couple of years, his self-driven entrepreneurial spirit kicked in and he struck out on his own. He rented a small office just a few doors away from Fox's, on the corner of Nassau Street and Grafton Street – a prestigious, central address just upstairs from another cigar shop, Kapp & Peterson. Needing to be the top listing in the phone book, he named his business 'Associated Agencies' (or 'AA' for short) and started seeking out niches in the market.

AMERICAN Magazines, the world famous "Life," alive in blazing colour and detail, each page a work of art. Avail of this opportunity to secure your copy all the year round. Regular and punctual delivery from America, post free, at only a nominal sum. This is a new post-war edition commencing next month and surpassing even the pre-war "Life." Also the American editions of Time and Fortune magazines. Full details from Joseph Murphy, 149 Thomas Street, Dublin. Phone 22891.

A small ad in *The Irish Press* from June 1946, when Joe was still trading from his home address.

In the years that followed, and with his sister Patricia serving as his secretary, Joe introduced Dubliners to all manner of new things – just like he had introduced exotic comic books to his schoolmates. He brought ballpoint pens – a recent innovation by Hungarian journalist László Bíró – into the country, as well as the glucose-infused orange drink Lucozade. With the ongoing war preventing the import of many fruits rich in vitamin C, Joe was the first to import Ribena – an English blackcurrant drink containing relatively high levels of the vitamin – into Ireland. Amongst the broad panoply of other products traded by AA were eggs, tea, chocolate, jam, and whatever other rare-during-wartime foodstuffs that Joe could get his hands on. He also created his own, cheaper version of a famous walnut-based chocolate treat; his version being called a 'Peanut Whip'. The cost of renting the office was £1 per week, and soon Joe was taking home around £10 per week, a modest yet sustainable wage.

Joe with wife Bunny in the early 50s. The pair met during
a 'Paul Jones' mixer dance in the Gresham Hotel.

JOE'S EUREKA MOMENT

In 1948, Joe married Bunny Boylan ('Bernadette' according to her birth cert, although nobody ever called her that) and they made their home in a small bungalow beside the Martello tower on Donabate strand. Joe was drawn to the sea, and kept himself fit by jogging and even handstand-walking along the strand. In the early 50s, on his drives home from work, he often stopped off at Savage's grocery shop in Swords village to pick up supplies for the family – which, by now, included toddler Yvonne and newborn Joe Jr. In addition to the basics like baby food and bread, he liked to grab a bag of crisps to help him along on the final leg of his journey. At that time, crisp packaging was still primitive and most crisps had made the journey from England, meaning that they weren't always as fresh as Joe would have liked. Having pointed out the staleness of the crisps to the shop-keeper on one too many occasions, Joe said that she retorted 'Well why in blazes don't you make them yourself, then?'

Mrs Savage could never have anticipated the impact that these words would go on to have. Joe went off and bought a recently published book by A. E. Williams, entitled *Potato Crisps: A Handbook for the Manufacturer and Others interested in the Economical Production of Potato Crisps*. This 106-page volume carried the seemingly excessive price tag of twenty-one shillings, but it gave Joe access to the author's thirty years of experience

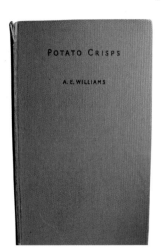

working as a chemist in the food industry. Within its pages, Joe learned everything about how to make crisps, from potato cultivation to storage and process-ing, and which equipment, oils and fats were required. Not only was this book an education, but it meant that Joe would never again have to hand over his hard-earned shillings in exchange for a flavourless, chewy bag of crisps. Not bad for twenty-one shillings, after all!

From these humble beginnings, Joe was about to produce his own unique brand of crisps, and in the process change Irish food forever.

THE BEGINNING
– 1954

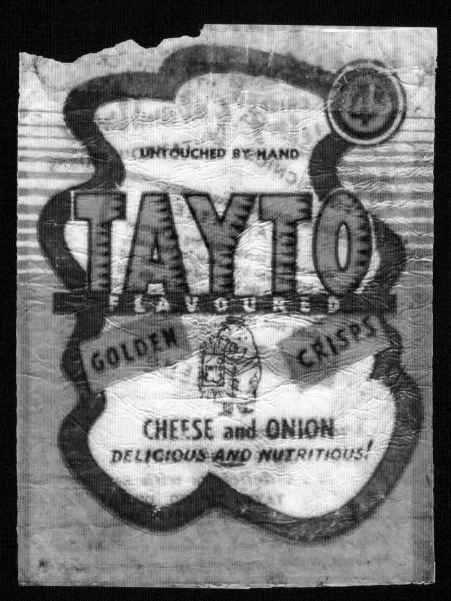

The oldest Tayto bag on record. This is almost identical to the original 1954 packets, apart from one key difference: Mr Tayto (although first introduced in 1955) was only added to the packaging at the beginning of the 60s.

O'RAHILLY PARADE

Soon after his Swords epiphany, at the age of thirty, Joe rented out a two-room premises on Dublin's O'Rahilly Parade for the princely sum of seventy shillings per week. Although it was only an unremarkable, shed-like structure, it was in the perfect location on the north side of the city – a few steps away from Moore Street (home to the city's oldest fruit and vegetable market), and just around the corner from the bustling main street of the capital. Within the two rooms of this premises, history was about to be made. Not that O'Rahilly Parade was any stranger to history. Formerly known as Sackville Lane, it had only recently been renamed in honour of Michael Joseph O'Rahilly (better known as The O'Rahilly) who died of a bullet wound in one of its doorways, on the last day of the Easter Rising. Joe, however, was about to make a *different* kind of history.

With a shoestring starting capital of just £500 (part of his inheritance), he was forced to rustle together a ragtag array of tools and equipment, from second-hand bathtubs to donated vegetable slicers and washcloths. Joe sourced his potatoes from a man named Lightfoot – one of the most experienced people in the potato trade – at the Dublin Corporation Wholesale Markets near St Mary's Abbey. Joe would have to take two trips over and back to the market, as he was going through four sacks of potatoes daily, but his humble Morris Minor could only fit two sacks at a time.

On the 26th of March 1954, the ramshackle crisp factory swung into operation. The potatoes were washed in a bathtub and then fed by hand into a slicer, one potato at a time. The slices were then washed again to remove the starch, before being dried in a clothes dryer and cooked in sunflower oil in one of two deep fat fryers, similar to those used in fish and chip shops around the country.

Though production had begun in earnest, Joe wasn't content to simply replicate the same crisps that crisp companies had been making for decades prior. Sure, his would be fresher – but ever the innovator, he wanted to offer more than just a bag of plain crisps with a sachet of salt included. He wanted to experiment with new flavours, and to find out if it was possible to give consumers crisps that they didn't have to season themselves. Like many of the best discoveries, this was an idea so perfect that – in hindsight – it seems remarkable that nobody thought of it before. Would it be possible to pre-flavour a bag of crisps? Enter Seamus Burke ...

THE SCIENTIST

Seamus Burke was a Sligo man, the third of six children born to Agnes and Malachy Burke. Born in 1918 (making him five years older than Joe), he spent the first four years of his life in Killala, before moving to Cloonacool, where he grew up in a house next door to Brennan's bar and shop. He attended Summerhill College in Sligo Town and was a member of the local amateur drama group, before leaving for London in his twenties. Upon his return to Ireland, he settled in Dublin, met Joe, and became one of Tayto's first four employees.

Around this time, Joe claimed that he 'hit on cheese and onion by accident.' He would later tell an interviewer, 'I had been doing a cheese flavour and an onion separately. One day I had too much onion flavouring ordered, and I got rid of it by mixing it in with the cheese.' Having stumbled upon this delicious pairing, Joe set Seamus the task of perfecting the measurements and ratios, concocting a recipe and – most important of all – figuring out how to get this flavour on to the crisps. Luckily, English bio-chemists Archer Martin and Richard Synge had just won the 1952 Nobel Prize in Chemistry, having invented a process called 'partition chromatography'. This had opened up a whole new world of possibilities when it came to flavouring food.

Using his kitchen table as his laboratory, Seamus got to work, throwing together common larder ingredients, in search of the winning combination. Ultimately, the flavouring process would

Cheese & Onion Flavour,
Special Mix

█████████████████████ } weigh into
█████████████████████   polythene bag
█████████████████████   with paper sack
                          outer. mark
                             SPECIAL

One of above mix to be added
to
████████████████████ = 2½ × 56 lb bags
████████████████████ = 10 × 14 lb castors
████████████████████ = 10 × 28 lb tins
84 lbs D.A.Y. = 3 × 28 lb bags
Method. Put flour & DAY into
mixer then add 1 special mix
run for 5 mins. Add salt +
█████████████████ + mix for about
10 minutes

Bourke
4/1/71

Seamus Burke's top secret recipe for *Tayto Cheese & Onion*.

begin with Seamus blending together several top-secret ingredients, then weighing around 20 kilograms of it into a polythene bag, which he would label with the word 'SPECIAL'. This SPECIAL mixture was then added to a mixer with *another* concoction that included flour, salt and onion powder. After fifteen minutes of mixing, he'd end up with 315 kilograms of cheese and onion flavouring, ready to mingle with – and adhere itself to – a batch of freshly fried potato slices. As if by magic, the iconic *Tayto Cheese & Onion* was born.

Seamus Burke in the midst of a research and development experiment.

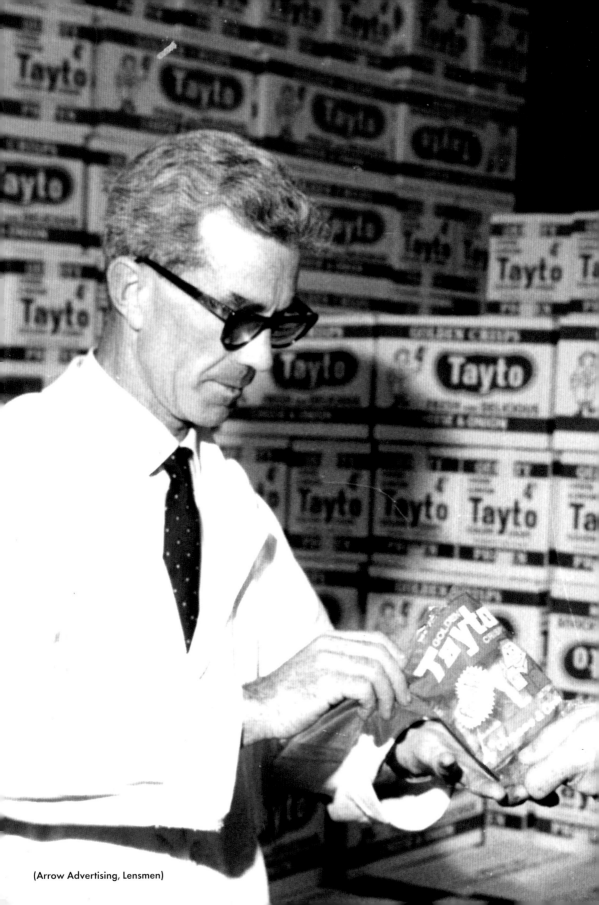

(Arrow Advertising, Lensmen)

THE LAUNCH

Burke's first impressions of his new workplace weren't exactly ideal. 'It was a dump', he remembered, 'but some of Mr. Murphy's enthusiasm must have rubbed off on me' – because upon being asked when he could start, Seamus answered – without a moment's hesitation – 'Now.' Joe handed him a copy of his now priceless A. E. Williams *Potato Crisps* book, and Seamus got straight to work. 'Like most people,' he said, 'I thought it was easy money.' To him, getting a few pence for a bag of crisps seemed like getting a few pence for a potato. 'I soon discovered that a hundredweight of potatoes didn't make a hundredweight of crisps. In fact, 80 per cent of weight was lost in the process.' And that's not to mention everything else involved in turning a seed potato into a flavoured crisp!

'It was a dump [...] but some of Mr. Murphy's enthusiasm must have rubbed off on me'

The cooked crisps were flavoured by hand and then packed into a waxed greaseproof paper bag, before being sealed by the company's first employee, Bernie Kane. Because Bernie had prior experience working in another crisp factory, Joe hired her and then immediately promoted her to assist him in recruitment. Bernie used to dip a paintbrush into a jam jar filled with glue, and then – according to Joe – 'seal the bag of crisps and admire it lovingly.' Like all of those early employees, and many other Tayto workers down through the years, Bernie continued working for the company for the rest of her career.

In need of a snappy name for his latest enterprise, Joe looked to his tiny namesake for inspiration. As an infant, Joe Jr had a particular fondness for potatoes and would often demand 'more taytos!' from his parents. His business-minded dad saw great branding potential in this charming mispronunciation, and so it was that Ireland's favourite eggcorn came into being.

After much practice, trial and error, Joe took out a small ad on the back page of *The Irish Times* on the 21st of May of that year. Buried amongst the ads for fireplaces, secondhand cars and a book entitled *Eternal Life: How to Possess It* was a far more earth-shattering discovery. This historic notice officially announced that 'from June 1st, your grocer has the new, deliciously flavoured Tayto Crisps'. The crisps – 'Full of goodness and lovely to taste' – came with an option of three flavours: Plain Golden Crisps, Cheese Flavour and Cheese-and-Onion Flavour.

FIRST ANNOUNCEMENT.

GOOD NEWS !

NEW.   NEW.

From June 1st your Grocer has the new. deliciously flavoured

TAYTO   CRISPS."

" Full of goodness and lovely to taste."

AND . . . IN 3 FLAVOURS :

Plain Golden Crisps.
Cheese flavour.
Cheese-and-onion flavour.

Only 4d. per packet.

Trade enquiries invited
(Free samples gladly sent without obligation).

——

THE TAYTO CRISP CO.

(Manufactured by Irish Food Exporters. Ltd.).

2 Dawson Street. Dublin.

Tel. 75108/9.

Joe already had an established relationship with upmarket wholesaler Findlater & Co, who had been selling many of his Associated Agencies products in more than twenty of their grocery outlets – including their flagship store beside the Parnell Monument on O'Connell Street, just around the corner from Tayto HQ. According to Dermot Findlater, the business of setting up Tayto had put Joe under serious financial strain – to the extent that Joe had even offered him half of the company in exchange for their backing. In a rather empathetic move, Dermot declined but pledged to help. Not only would they promote Tayto in all of their stores, but Joe's wife Bunny would be allowed to shop in their Malahide branch on credit, until Tayto had gotten off the ground. This came as a huge lifeline to Joe – and Dermot wouldn't be long waiting for payment. Findlater also employed a number of sales representatives – then known as 'commercial travellers' – to distribute their wares to other independent retailers. With Findlater on board, Tayto Crisps were soon available in shops all across the country, including Savage's grocery shop on Swords Main Street, where the original idea had been born.

A tin of Cheese & Onion from the early days of Tayto. Each tin held eighteen packets of crisps.

'I felt on top of
the world when,
on my second day,
we produced thirty-
five tins of crisps
after nine hours
of hard slogging!'

SEAMUS BURKE

HITTING THE GROUND RUNNING

At the factory, eighteen packets of crisps would be packed into a large airtight tin, to help to maintain their freshness. This tin would then be sold to shops for four shillings, plus a refundable two-shilling deposit on the tin itself, with shops outside of Dublin charged an additional half-shilling to cover the additional travel expenses. Each bag of crisps came with a price tag of fourpence emblazoned on the front, giving the retailer slightly more than a penny and a farthing of profit for each packet sold.

With eighteen packets of crisps per tin, this amounted to the production of 630 packs over a long day's work. An output of just more than one pack per minute wasn't bad to begin with, but it would soon prove to be unsustainable. By the end of June, Joe would be placing ads in the newspapers, stating that they urgently required 'girls with experience of fish frying or similar work'.

Harry Murray was the first member of the sales team – a team that, within a year or so, would expand to include Paddy Lynch, Gerry Sweeney and Paddy Lillis. In the early days, before Tayto could afford vans, they used to set out from O'Rahilly Parade on foot – and they weren't always met with a red carpet wherever they went. Some shopkeepers were weary of buying in any crisps, due to the fact that their former crisp supplier had gone bust a couple of years prior, leaving them with shelves full of stale, unwanted stock. Seamus theorized that the reason for the once-successful company's collapse had been because they 'got too greedy and packed all sorts of crap, with sad results', their downfall perhaps providing the nascent Tayto with some lessons to learn from. Another reason for the reluctance of some shopkeepers was because of the extra two shillings they were expected to pay for the tin. Even though this was only a deposit, some saw it as a hassle they could do without. However, the combination of a pioneering product and a charming sales team won through in the end.

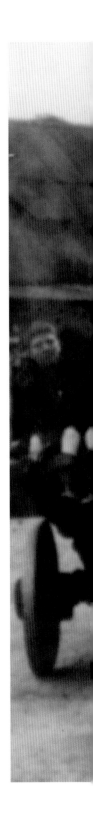

Joe (second from left, standing) and colleagues
accepting a delivery of potatoes to O'Rahilly Parade.

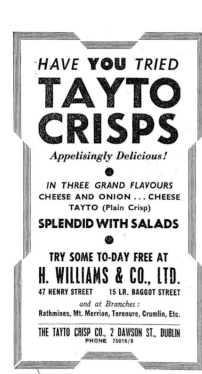

HAVE **YOU** TRIED
TAYTO CRISPS

Appetisingly Delicious!

●

IN THREE GRAND FLAVOURS
CHEESE AND ONION ... CHEESE
TAYTO (Plain Crisp)

SPLENDID WITH SALADS

●

TRY SOME TO-DAY FREE AT
H. WILLIAMS & CO., LTD.
47 HENRY STREET   15 LR. BAGGOT STREET
and at Branches :
Rathmines, Mt. Merrion, Terenure, Crumlin, Etc.

THE TAYTO CRISP CO., 2 DAWSON ST., DUBLIN
PHONE 75018/9

Some of Tayto's earliest advertisements, including one cheeky notice – from a Cork distributor – during the bread shortage of 1954.

BREAD STRIKE

TAYTO CRISPS will more than make up for the shortage of bread.   They are in three delicious flavours, Cheese and Onion, Cheese and Plain with Salt.   Ask your grocer, shop, or licensed house Trade enquiries to agents

F. CADE and SONS LTD.,
SOUTH TERRACE, CORK

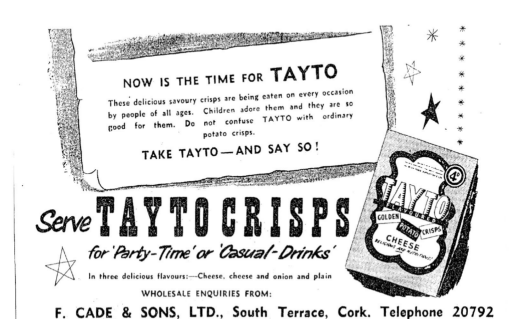

NOW IS THE TIME FOR **TAYTO**

These delicious savoury crisps are being eaten on every occasion by people of all ages. Children adore them and they are so good for them. Do not confuse TAYTO with ordinary potato crisps.

TAKE TAYTO — AND SAY SO !

Serve **TAYTO CRISPS**

for 'Party-Time' or 'Casual-Drinks'

In three delicious flavours:—Cheese, cheese and onion and plain

WHOLESALE ENQUIRIES FROM:

F. CADE & SONS, LTD., South Terrace, Cork. Telephone 20792

This 1955 ad notably features an illustration of the very first ever Tayto packet.

It wasn't long before customer demand had outgrown both Tayto's resources and their equipment. For a start, they used to dry the potato slices in a domestic spin dryer designed to dry a few damp T-shirts every couple of days, not a constant cycle of kilos upon kilos of soaking wet potatoes. 'It very often took off from its moorings and flew around the room,' according to Seamus. 'Luckily, no one was ever hurt by it.'

In these early days, most of the profits made were invested back into the company. This allowed the company to achieve constant growth without resorting to outside funding, at a time when the banks were hesitant to lend to fledgling enterprises. Soon, Joe was able to invest in upgrading their production chain, through the acquirement of some high-tech machinery like a packing machine and a spiral elevator. Advancements like this helped to increase their output from thirty-five tins per day to 1,000 tins per day!

Despite this, it had become increasingly difficult to keep up with demand from within the confines of the two rooms on O'Rahilly Parade – and the higgledy-piggledy, DIY production facility was ill befitting of a respectable, successful company. The notoriously image-conscious Joe knew how important it was to look professional, which is why he made sure to have embossed notepaper, an early telex machine and several phone lines instead of just one. This is why he would later admit, 'I was not proud of that factory. Customers and other people used to ask to see the factory. After all, making potato chips was something new in Ireland in those days, but I just couldn't let them see it. I had to make all kinds of excuses.'

August 1955 saw the incorporation of Tayto Ltd. With the crisp-making enterprise now established as a separate entity from Joe's other business pursuits, it was high time for Tayto to ramp up production, further professionalize its setup, and take things to the next level.

RATHMINES
– 1955

SOUTHSIDE EXPANSION

The establishment of a new factory in the Southside suburb of Rathmines — then known as 'Flatland', as many of its grand town-houses had been subdivided into tiny flats — made sense for a number of reasons. While still remaining close to town, rents were cheaper on the outskirts, allowing Joe to secure a larger premises. Being away from the hustle and bustle of the city centre also meant that parking — as well as loading/unloading thousands of tins every day — would be that bit easier. And last, but probably not least, Joe's commute to work would be shortened ever so slightly. The Murphys had now officially entered into the upper echelons of Irish society, with a move to Glenageary — and driving to Rathmines instead of the Northside meant avoiding the trek across town and the Liffey.

At 38C Upper Mountpleasant Avenue (where the Mount Pleasant Business Centre now stands), Tayto was soon capable of producing 3,500 tins per day — more than 100 times the amount that Seamus Burke had been so proud of making on his second day, just over a year earlier. The introduction of an expensive gum-sealing unit meant that Bernie Kane could retire her paintbrush and tub of glue, to instead take up a job elsewhere along the conveyor belt. Members of the sales team no longer had to set out at the crack of dawn with a tin each under their arm, as they now had access to a fleet of ten vans. At a time when most commercial vehicles simply had the company's name written on the side, each Tayto van was painted with an eye-catching, multicolour display that no pedestrian or fellow motorist could miss.

(LEFT) One of the new, top-of-the-range fryers in the Rathmines factory. (Irish Photo Archive/Lensmen Collection)

Apology

Tayto Crisps apologise for being unable to meet the demands of the hundreds of new customers who have written for supplies.

However, we are now in a position to supply new customers direct in the Dublin City area, and in the country through our distributors.

TAYTO LIMITED

RATHMINES, DUBLIN

Telephones: 95597 and 44511

In September 1955, with the new factory firing on all cylinders, Joe issued an apology to the shopkeepers of Ireland. For months, Tayto had been flying off the shelves faster than they could be stocked. Joe hoped that the 63,000 packets of crisps made every day in Rathmines would be enough to appease the newly crisp-addicted masses.

The October of that year, Joe placed a small notice in the *Belfast Telegraph*, inviting enquiries from any Belfast wholesalers who might wish to become his Northern Irish distribution partner. Unfortunately, the hard border of the time made it difficult – if not impossible – to achieve his ambition of making his crisps available in all thirty-two counties. Instead, an Armagh business-man named Thomas Hutchinson made him an offer for a license to manufacture his own crisps up north, using the already famous Tayto name. In need of the capital to keep expanding his business, Joe accepted this deal and the rest, as they say, is history.

THE DAWN OF A CULTURAL ICON

Nothing can gauge the pulse of the Irish nation quite like a pantomime. At Christmastime 1956, a Cork production of *Babes in the Wood* centred around three thieves named Doughnut, Popcorn and Tayto – evidence of how quickly Tayto had entered into the national consciousness, as well as the snack Hall of Fame. Tayto's growing popularity, and with it their large-scale consumption of the Irish potato crop, quickly came to the attention of the national press. Writing in the agricultural pages of *The Irish Times* that winter, journalist James Gilbert commended 'a new Irish industry that uses our own farm produce as its basic raw material, and which is making a smashing success out of it.' Clarifying who he was referring to, he continued:

> This is "Tayto Ltd.", makers of those appetising potato crisps which maybe you've come across. This firm only started up a couple of years ago, and in a very small way. One ton of spuds a week was all they used for the first four months. Now they take in over thirty tons a week. They're expanding fast, but they can't satisfy the growing demand – because they are turning out a first-class product which can stand up to, and surpass, competition anywhere. I foresee a big future for them in the export trade – and a very useful outlet for our potatoes as well.

An early Tayto van,
painted by Clondalkin
signwriter Leo Darbey.
(Anne Darbey/
the Darbey family)

Gilbert, elaborating upon perfectionist Joe's quest for blight-free potatoes, then inadvertently suggested a nickname for the Tayto boss that would follow him around for the rest of his life.

> A point of considerable interest is this: Joe (Spud?) Murphy, the founder and driving force behind Tayto, says they have been getting a very high proportion of potatoes that looked excellent but which were blight-blackened inside. The dark marks seemed, to me, to make no difference to the edibility of the crisp, but they won't do for Joe Murphy. They have to be hand-picked for these blemishes. Only the best, etc. In consequence, there has been a tremendous amount of waste. If Tayto Ltd. could count on getting potatoes completely free of these "blight stains", they would pay very well for them. So over to you.

In his same column the following week, Gilbert seems to have made the executive decision that his new nickname for Joe should stick, reporting – without any question marks, this time – that 'Mr. "Spud" Murphy, of Tayto Crisps, says that his firm will also pay premium prices for properly graded and genuinely clean Kerr's Pinks. Any takers?' And so it was that 'Spud' was born – although the media and others would more often refer to him as 'Tayto Murphy'.

31st January 1958: Tins of Tayto are loaded into a van parked outside the factory in Rathmines. (Irish Photo Archive/Lensmen Collection)

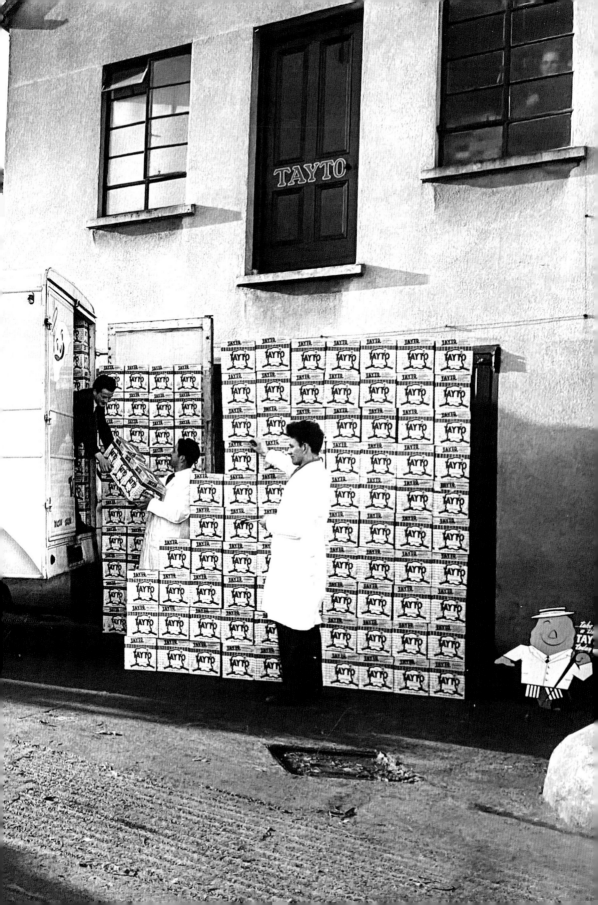

It was a far more complicated industry than Joe ever expected [...] they had to figure everything out for themselves.

EVERY DAY'S A SCHOOL DAY

Spud's insistence on Kerr's Pink spuds – originally grown in Scotland – was the consequence of years of experimentation with different varieties of potato, including Arran Banner, Arran Pilot, Arran Victory and Maris Piper. He and his team had found that the crisps that they made differed greatly depending on which potatoes had been used in their production. Kerr's Pink potatoes – with their pink skin, creamy white flesh, and dry, floury texture – had provided the most satisfying results, but unfortunately they also happened to have a low resistance to blight.

This wasn't the only knowledge that the freshly anointed potato experts at Tayto had acquired. They learned that frost destroyed the crisping potential of potatoes. They also learned that the quality of the finished product was heavily dependent on slice thickness, the cooking temperature, and even how the sacks of raw potatoes had been handled during the transportation process. It was a far more complicated industry than Joe ever expected and, as the only crisp company in the country, they had to figure everything out for themselves. Every day was a school day.

Eventually, Joe was able to put together a reliable Rolodex of potato growers and merchants that could keep his factories well supplied. His main supplier would be Balbriggan farmer Maurice McAuley, whose son Edmund would later inherit the family farm and continue to supply potatoes to Tayto into the 21st century. The musician Philip Chevron – a member of The Pogues and The Radiators From Space – often spoke about his Grandfather LaGrue, who was a potato trader in the Dublin Corporation Wholesale Markets near Smithfield. LaGrue supplied potatoes to Tayto, which Chevron said was 'one of the big contracts you could get at the time'. This contract helped LaGrue to upgrade his family from the working class to the middle class, enabling a move from the densely populated urban chaos of The Liberties to a bigger house in the well-heeled suburb of Terenure.

A pub sign from the 1950s, reminding drinkers that sustenance was available behind the bar! (Enya Barron)

TWO YEARS A-GROWIN'

The LaGrues weren't the only ones eyeing up property in the Terenure area. Remarkably, Tayto managed to outgrow its Rathmines factory in less than two years and, by the beginning of 1957, Joe was on the hunt for *another* additional building – preferably a 'ground floor factory premises' of 'ten to twelve thousand square feet', with 'all services and preferably a modern building.' He somehow managed to find exactly what he was looking for on Tivoli Avenue, right between Terenure and Harold's Cross.

Around this time, in March 1957, Joe also had to pay a visit to the Four Courts. Three Dundrum residents – Sarah, William and Catherine Tracey – had obviously taken note of the insatiable public demand for Tayto, and had decided to start making their own crisps. The problem? They had named their ones 'Tatto Crisps', with the word 'TATTO' featuring prominently on the packaging and tins. Joe applied for an injunction to prevent them from using this trading style, 'or any other style so closely resembling Tayto Ltd. as to confuse the public' or 'in such a way as to pass off their goods for the plaintiffs' goods.' The case was settled, and the Traceys agreed to retire the Tatto brand. They say imitation is the best form of flattery, but this may have been a bit *too* flattering for Joe.

In between lawsuits, property-hunting and setting up a new factory, Joe somehow found time to issue more heartfelt apologies to his loyal customers through the national press.

Important Announcement

TAYTO CRISPS

- Due to the unprecedented nation-wide demand for TAYTO Crisps, we are, in the present circumstances, unable to fulfil all orders.

- We wish to apologise to all those who have failed to get their orders completed (especially our country customers), and assure them that, despite increasing production by 300%, we are still unable to meet all requirements for TAYTO.

- Plans for another TAYTO factory (our third) are well in hand, and we hope that this, coupled with the extension of our present factories, will enable us to fully satisfy demands within the next two months— meanwhile we shall be still obliged to ration TAYTO until mid-September.

TAYTO, LTD., RATHMINES, DUBLIN

IMPORTANT ANNOUNCEMENT

TAYTO LTD. wish to apologise to the TRADE and PUBLIC for a temporary shortage of everybody's favourite,—

T A Y T O.

Due to the present bad quality of the potatoes, i.e., finish of old crop, we prefer to cut down our production, as our TRADE MARK—T A Y T O, is your guarantee of quality always, and in endeavouring to keep this standard, we are using over FORTY TONS of potatoes per week. However, our Contracts for New Potatoes commence on July 1st, and by July 4th there should be increased supplies for everybody . . . until then please bear with us.

OUR SPECIAL THANKS TO THE TRADE FOR THEIR CONSISTENT CO-OPERATION.

Newspaper notices taken out by Joe in 1956 and 1957, demonstrating some of the difficulties faced by Tayto during its infancy.

NEWSPAPER
ADVERTISING

everyone knows
that the Irish
for crisps is
Tayto

TAYTO IN THE BROADSHEETS

During its formative years, Tayto relied heavily on national, local and regional newspaper advertising to get the word out about the revolutionary new crisp on the scene. With a seven-year gap between the introduction of Tayto and the arrival of domestic television in Ireland, print advertising was still king. With the 'small ads' on the back page of many newspapers functioning as a community notice board of sorts, it was the only way for a brand to land itself on every breakfast table, bus to work and office desk in the land.

3

WINNERS

from the

TAYTO

    Stable

1st for the 11 o'clock
    TAYTO Plain

1st for the 4 o'clock
    TAYTO Cheese

1st for the Bona Fide Stakes
    TAYTO Cheese and Onion

People who Know

    Buy Tayto

At this time, it was still common for advertisements to be accompanied by illustrations, which would largely be phased out in favour of photographs in the proceeding years. After Tayto's 'First Announcement – Good News!' declaration of existence in May 1954, a number of low-budget text ads followed.

In October 1955, Tayto launched its first illustrated ad, which simultaneously appeared in almost every newspaper in Ireland, from *The Kerryman* to the *Westmeath Independent*, and from the *Connacht Tribune* to *The Munster Express*. The ad featured a shopkeeper telling his customer about the latest sensation to hit the shelves – as well as perhaps insinuating that he likes to pair his Tayto with something stronger than milk. This drawing would be used as a template over the next couple of years, repurposed with a different caption every time.

(OPPOSITE) The pupils in this 1960s classroom are probably asking 'An bhfuil cead agam paicéad Tayto a ithe?'

(LEFT) A horseracing-themed ad, as featured in the *Trinity News* in May 1955.

Mr Tayto made his debut appearance in this ad from October 1955.

Nestled at the bottom of this ad was a small line drawing of a dapperly dressed anthropomorphic potato man, sporting a broad grin and holding a packet of Tayto. Although still nameless at this point, this was the unceremonious debut of somebody that would go on to much bigger things. More on him later.

Many of these early ads contained serving suggestions, in a bid to convince consumers that a packet of Tayto was exactly the thing that their recipes had been missing all along. There were ads in *The Irish Press* ('Tayto are wonderful at any time – particularly with the breakfast fry.'), the *Evening Herald* ('Have you tried Tayto Crisps? Splendid with salads.') and the *Irish Independent* ('Tayto are tops. The youngsters go for them in a big way with sausages and tomatoes.'). No dish existed that wouldn't be vastly improved with the addition of a handful of crunchy, flavourful Tayto.

An early Tayto
obsessive, as depicted
in November 1955.

Rounding off the menu the following month, the next illustration
assured the reader that Tayto are 'Wonderful as a supper snack
with a glass of milk.' This ad depicted a grinning, somewhat shifty
gentleman, leaning out from behind the neighbouring column.
The man claims to be running out of the house to grab a packet of
Cheese & Onion before the shops close, but first he finds time to
deliver a hasty pro-Tayto monologue to his partner.

Joe quickly realized that hungry, busy students would be another
prime audience for his wares, and so he started taking out
specially tailored ads in the *Trinity News*. In the first such
placement, we meet the same shopkeeper and customer as
before. This time, however, the customer is a university lecturer
complaining about his Tayto-addicted students. The shopkeeper
is able to offer little in the way of a solution, instead advising the
professor to join the ranks of the crisp-eating hordes. It seems that
resistance to Tayto is futile, as far as he is concerned.

CRISP THINKING

In November 1959, the world was on the cusp of the Golden Age of Advertising, an era that would see ads constantly competing to be as big, bold, brash and in-your-face as possible. Not so for Joe, who took this as the ideal moment to revert back to good old-fashioned personal ads. Hidden in amongst the job listings and lonely hearts columns, 'Crisp Thinking' was a series of short four-line poems with an ABCB rhyming pattern. Each of these quaint little ballad stanzas focused on a different type of worker (a bus conductor, a lorry driver, a window cleaner, etc.), suggesting how Tayto might improve their working life and help them to get through the day.

Although the provenance of these poems is unknown, the concept – if not the verses themselves – almost certainly came from Joe. A lover of language, words and poetry (especially the short stories of O. Henry, and *The Green Eye of the Yellow God* by J. Milton Hayes, of which he could recite large sections off by heart), he scribbled illegible notes on every blank patch of paper in the house, from book margins to packing cardboard. He kept

---

" CRISP THINKING "

Lorry drivers out all day,

Going to places far and near,

Lay in stocks of TAYTO CRISPS,

For making sure they're in top gear !

" CRISP THINKING "

Policemen clearing traffic jams,

Find it wearing on the feet.

Why not give them Special Duty—

Like lots of TAYTO CRISPS to eat ?

" CRISP THINKING "

Postmen on their early round

Must often feel they'd like a snack.

As well as letters, TAYTO CRISPS

Should be in every postman's sack !

A series of poems that appeared in the newspapers in November 1959.

a notepad and pen by his bedside, to jot down dreams and late-night ideas, and would often say to his kids, 'Whatever the idea/ No matter how bright/Always put it down in black and white.'

As we entered the 60s, Tayto's newspaper ads became less frequent as Joe turned his focus to other avenues of exposure, including radio, TV and sponsorship. The print ads had largely served their purpose for Tayto, having helped the company to introduce itself to the public and establish the playful, honest and friendly brand identity that it wished to maintain.

The newspapers had also given Joe a direct line to people all over Ireland, so that he could provide production updates and apologies – if need be – as Tayto scambled to streamline its supply chain. And of course, Tayto would continue to use the newspapers for job listings and public service announcements. Having won the attention – and hearts – of the Irish public, it was now time to maintain this attention whilst engaging with people in other ways.

"CRISP THINKING"

Bus conductors' ups and downs

Would be less tiring if they tried

Before the bus starts off at all—

TAYTO CRISPS inside!

"CRISP THINKING"

Window cleaners often feel

That life is just an endless pane.

With TAYTO CRISPS to cheer them up,

They'd never feel that way again!

"CRISP THINKING"

Housewives have a hectic life

Cooking, washing, sewing.

Without a break for TAYTO CRISPS

They couldn't keep on going!

HAROLD'S CROSS
– 1957

(ABOVE) In 1959, Tayto ran the 'Tayto Display Competition For Licensed Premises', offering a first prize of £40 to the publicans who could put together the best Tayto display. Pictured here is the valiant effort of The Harbour Bar in Bray... which somehow *didn't* win the prize.

(RIGHT) An ad published to coincide with St Patrick's Day 1962. Tayto regularly won prizes – for advertising through Irish – at the annual Glór na nGael competition, which was founded by Cumann na Sagart (The Association of Irish-Speaking Priests).

'T' FOR 'TAYTO'

The huge new factory, at 11A Tivoli Avenue, was only a five-minute drive west of the Rathmines plant. It was also, handily enough, just up the road from the Bailey Gibson paper mill on the South Circular Road, where Tayto sourced its packaging material. Tayto had what now amounted to a sprawling crisp empire in the leafy south suburbs. The local kids of Harold's Cross – intoxicated by the smell of fresh crisps wafting across the area – were especially delighted, gladly helping themselves to what they referred to as 'tit-bits' from the barrel of waste left outside the front door of the factory.

largest manufacturers of cheese and onion crisps in the world—TAYTO are Irish right through, and proud of their product, their people, and their popularity. Over 37 million bags sold in 1961 in Ireland alone.

Bíodh agat leithéidí seamróg nó sailéillel
Ach ná bí i bponc ar ócáid na féile—
Do Lá Fhéile Pádraig, faigh TAYTO go leor...
'S le bheith dearfa cinnte de ... méadaigh do stól

As well as growing in a business sense, Tayto was also growing as a community and garnering a reputation as an attractive place to work, and as a company that treated its employees fairly. A typical Tayto job listing of the time promised top rates, good canteen facilities, and even 'music while you work'. In 1957, the sausage salesmen of Donnelly Meats were granted a pay rise of ten shillings, prompting the Tayto salesmen to approach Joe to ask for a similar increase. Believing *his* salesmen to be the best in the country, Joe gave them a raise of twice the amount that they were looking for – an extra pound per week. Workers could also look forward to the annual summer outing – a bus trip to somewhere like picturesque Delgany or Brittas Bay in Wicklow, to enjoy some fresh air, live music and a few drinks. The Christmas Ball – held in the Rathmines canteen – brought with it such excitement that one eyewitness raved about it being 'positively supercharged', with 'a gladiatorial air to the proceedings' as staff danced to rock and roll on the gramophone.

One of the original team, Matty Duane, kept a close eye on his salesmen and would quiz anyone that returned at the end of the day with so much as one unsold tin. 'Did you go off to the pictures instead?' he'd ask them, only half-jokingly. Another early employee, Paddy Lillis, once drove to Dundalk on Christmas Eve, to deliver eighty tins to a wholesaler that needed them urgently. Upon his return to base, Lillis was met by Joe, who was so impressed by his dedication that he handed him £40 in cash – the equivalent of around a month's wage.

For its first few years in business, Tayto packed and distributed crisps in the aforementioned metal tins. This resulted in them needing to purchase a tin-washing machine. As sales increased, the tins became less and less efficient, as considerable time and labour was lost in unloading and handling empties from the vans, before cleaning, drying and refilling them. Packing an extra two packets of crisps into each tin did little to ease the pressure. The eventual decision to make the switch to cartons was a net positive for the company's accountants and packers – but the sales team were soon receiving complaints about stale crisps, which had never happened before, during the tin era. They solved this problem by lining the cartons with polythene bags, which in turn created a new expense and more work for the packers. Despite years of progress and success, the team was still having to figure out things as they went along.

TAYTO

the best part of a good meal!

Public Opinion demands **tayto**

and still only costs 4d.

"Cheese & Onion" flavoured TAYTO a treat for young and old

A BAGFUL OF NOURISHMENT

Only the choicest selected top grade potatoes are used in the manufacture of Tayto Crisps

that's why **TAYTO** are terrific

TAYTO crisps

(LEFT) A Tayto Christmas party from the late 50s. Bernie Kane is in the front row, second from right; Seamus Burke is beside her, third from right.

TAYTO *Ltd.* RATHMINES · DUBLIN · IRELAND

Phone:
95597 AND 92677

MEMBER NATIONAL POTATO CHIP INSTITUTE U.S.A.

● MANUFACTURERS & PACKERS OF SAVOURY SPECIALITIES ●

BANKERS:
MUNSTER & LEINSTER BANK LTD
GRAFTON STREET, DUBLIN

OUR REF   JMM/UC

YOUR REF

DATE 11th July, 1957.

CONFIDENTIAL MEMO

to   Mr. Seamus Bourke

Dear Mr. Bourke,

It gives me much pleasure to send you the enclosed little cheque with my Compliments and Thanks for the excellent work which you have consistently carried out in our ORGANIZATION, perhaps, I can be forgiven if I mention more particularly, your unceasing efforts in TIVOLI AVE..........

I am now looking forward to being in a position to give you a considerable increase in salary as you shall be carrying the major responsibility of our three ramifications, i.e.,

TIN WASHING BAY
FLAVOURING BAY
SIZE-ABLE PRODUCTION UNIT.

I hope to put this into effect before the year is out.

In fullest appreciation of your integrity, conscientiousness, and consistent co-operation at all times.

Yours faithfully,
TAYTO LTD.

JOSEPH M. MURPHY.

(ABOVE) Some Tayto staff members enjoying what was an early Tayto tradition – the annual staff outing, this one being down to Delgany in County Wicklow. Another staff tradition, some years later, was for a bride-to-be to don a sombrero with Tayto packets dangling from it, with more Tayto bags pinned to her dress. She was then pushed around the factory in a wheelbarrow, before being taped to a pole in the yard until a manager noticed that she was missing – hopefully with enough time to spare before her big day. (Irish Photo Archive)

(LEFT) Joe's 1957 letter to Seamus Burke, notifying him of a promotion and pay increase.

so clean!

NO WASTE, NO WORK
NO WORRY WITH
TAYTOPAK
graded potatoes
top quality

TAYTOPAK

TRADE INQUIRIES: TAYTO LTD. RATHMINES, DUBLIN 6.

O'Keeffes

even size
for even
cooking

1/-

Listen to "Leisure Time"
on Radio Eireann every
Tuesday at 3.45 p.m.

for even tempers

Cut cooking time and save yourself
troublesome preparation by *insisting* on
P.D.L. Potatoes. Hand graded and cleaned,
of even size for even cooking, a shilling
pack of these top quality potatoes ensures
a *two day* supply for the average family!
They save scraping and scrubbing too
because, packed in handy polythene packs,
they're cleaner, and quicker to cook!
Why take pot luck when you can have
a money back guaranteed pack of perfect
Potatoes — tested by TAYTO.

**look for the Mr. Tayto
trade mark on every pack**

POTATO DISTRIBUTORS LIMITED. · HAROLD'S CROSS. · DUBLIN. · TEL. 90017

Newspaper advertisements for one of Joe's potato-based side projects:
The TaytoPak. The 'Even Size For Even Cooking' ad, from 1959, marked the
very first time that the company's mascot was referred to as 'Mr. Tayto'.

TAYTOPAK

Once both factories were operating at full capacity, Tayto had worked out most of the kinks faced by any new company undergoing rapid growth during a period of unprecedented success. In 1959, with supply and production both stable, Joe finally had the time, resources and potatoes available to turn his attention to a new pet project, setting up a subsidiary of Tayto called Potato Distributors Ltd.

Until this point, grocers had most commonly sold potatoes in large burlap sacks containing around a half-tonne of potatoes pulled straight from the earth and covered in soil. Joe hit upon the idea of selling hand-graded, pre-washed potatoes in handy bags only a fraction of the regular size. This pound bag of potatoes – dubbed the 'TaytoPak' – sold for a shilling (twelve pence) and enticed shoppers with taglines like 'Even Size For Even Cooking For Even Tempers', and the far snappier 'MORE SPUD LESS MUD'. Each bag also carried a money-back guarantee; if the customer was dissatisfied with the quality of their pack, they could return it for a refund or replacement.

The TaytoPak was a huge success, but crisps were always Joe's number one priority – especially during times that potatoes were in short supply. In the years that followed, Joe was sometimes forced – as if stuck in a loop – to turn down new customers or implement a quota system to ration stock. At one stage, he even offered to send desperate retailers an unbranded half tonne bag of potatoes. The TaytoPak had come full circle.

'I had to give it up,' Joe later reflected. 'Quite frankly, making potato chips was more profitable than making housewives' packs – and I needed every inch of space for that.' A few decades later, the concept of pre-cleaned/pre-peeled/pre-cooked potatoes would be a huge global industry. It perhaps could be argued that Joe helped to pave the way for the many convenience potato products on supermarket shelves today – but back then he had plenty of other things on his plate.

PETE'S PEANUTS

Around the same time that Joe brought the TaytoPak to the market, he also introduced Ireland to Tayto's first non-potato offering. For the name of this product, he once again looked to one of his children for inspiration – and so, Pete's Peanuts was named in honour of his third son, Peter. Joe started buying raw peanuts in bulk, via an importer down on the quays of the Liffey. They were then roasted in a chip pan, salted and packed into bags, a process overseen by the company's new production manager, Des Kavanagh. Pete's Peanuts were available in two size options: a small three-penny bag and a larger six-penny bag. The bagged peanuts were initially sold to the retailer in boxes, but Tayto later followed the example of a rival peanut company and started attaching the peanut packets to hangable card strips.

Just like every Tayto packet featured a friendly, unprocessed, anthropomorphic potato, each bag of Pete's featured a friendly, unprocessed, anthropomorphic peanut – a jolly monkey nut wearing a cowboy hat, equipped with a gun, holster and lasso. It was the Golden Age of the Western and gunslingers were very much in fashion, with John Wayne and James Stewart on the silver screen and even our own local hero Bang Bang roaming the streets of Dublin. Tayto leaned further into this cowboy theme with the slogan 'Don't Never Go Nowhere Without 'Em!', as well as the slightly less American, slightly more forceful tagline, 'EVERYBODY EATS PETE'S PEANUTS'. A TV commercial for Pete's Peanuts showed Pete – speaking in a thick cowboy drawl – declining an array of typical cowboy foods, opting instead for a packet of his own nuts:

"They're roastier, toastier, tastier too. You can keep all your flapjacks, your beans, your black coffee. When I feel like eatin', it's Pete's that I chew!"

THE SWINGING 60S

The 1960s was a monumental decade, not just in Ireland, but across the world. As the hangover from the Second World War finally began to subside, it brought with it huge technological advancements, cultural shifts and an economic boom. The snack food market started to increase at an even faster pace than before. Supermarkets and convenience store chains became more widespread and were significantly larger than the previously commonplace grocery shops. The arrival of television opened up a whole new way of advertising, and glued-to-the-screen, square-eyed viewers needed something to munch on. So did the socializers in the growing number of cool new lounge bars across our cities. Back then, it was rare for an Irish pub to sell food, but now publicans had a full range of handy little packets to offer their clientele, that could help to stave off hunger and keep them drinking for a little while longer. It had even become common enough for Tayto to be served as a decadent side dish, sometimes served warm, alongside game and other cold meats – perhaps inspired by some of Joe's earliest ads.

Ireland's nascent snack and confectionery market had initially been regarded as the sole preserve of children, but suddenly people of all ages were enjoying the occasional treat ... and antipasto. Tayto found itself in the right place at the right time, ready to make the most of this exciting new era.

PARTYGIVERS...
PARTYGOERS...

Add an extra appetising touch to party time ... cocktail time ... the tangy taste of golden TAYTO Crisps served as a side dish ... to go so well with every kind of drink ... every kind of occasion that calls for specially good standards in perfect party fare.

A

HAPPY AND

PROSPEROUS

NEW YEAR

to all our

friends and customers

from

TAYTO Ltd.

Over 35,000,000 (thirty-five million) bags eaten and enjoyed in Ireland during 1961.

100% Irish capital and 100% Irish labour.

Éillíonn aigne an pnobail Cayto

A notice placed in *The Irish Times* on New Year's Day, 1962.

EXPANDING FURTHER AFIELD

It had only been a few short years since Joe was having to drive over and back to the Smithfield market, in his Morris Minor, to pick up a few sacks of potatoes. Now his company was going through more than 3,000 tonnes of potatoes every year, and they weren't ready to stop there. A few days into the New Year and there was *another* listing in the same paper, this time looking for even more staff. This particular ad was both an excellent opportunity for girls *and* distinctly of its time.

SITUATIONS VACANT

Excellent opportunity for
GIRLS

Tayto Ltd. are still expanding and require Senior and Junior Girls for their Rathmines and also their Harold's Cross Factories. Excellent working conditions, trade union rates, canteen facilities, five day week. Reply by letter only, stating experience, to the Works Manager.

TAYTO LTD.
RATHMINES, DUBLIN

A 1962 job listing.

As was the norm with the majority of companies at that time, the offices of Tayto were mostly populated by men (aside from receptionist Mary O'Herlihy and Joe's secretary Sylvia Cushen). Of course, the rest of the female staff members were all out on the factory floor, actually making the crisps. Furthermore, Joe's eldest son, Joe Jr, would later give a huge amount of the credit for Tayto's success to another woman: his mother, Bunny. 'She is a terrific hostess', he said, 'and managed to make all of Dad's most important customers feel right at home. She was as beautiful as any model and she was into relationship marketing before the term had been invented. Dad could be tough, but she has all the social graces.'

The TAYTO Depot Staff in Cork combine together as they say "We wish our TAYTO customers a happy joyous Christmas Day! A New Year of prosperity, packed with health and fortune too— from Mary, Michael, both the Pats this wish is sent to all of you!"

TAYTO LIMITED
12 LR. BUCKINGHAM PLACE
GEORGE'S QUAY, CORK

(ABOVE) An example of the new, improved, polythene-lined cartons that eventually replaced the tins.

(LEFT) A Christmas greeting placed in a local newspaper by the management at the Cork depot.

In 1962, Tayto saw the need to start opening depots dotted around the country. They already had one in Cork (opened in 1960), but soon there was another in Limerick, quickly followed by more in Galway, Cavan, Sligo and Donegal. Despite being set up and ready to go on schedule, the opening of the Galway depot had to be delayed due to, somewhat predictably, a shortage of stock. After six weeks or so of waiting, the depot could finally begin distributing snacks to shops all over Connaught. Although there were still occasionally some brief periods of undersupply like this, Tayto eventually started catching up with the incredible demand for their products, to the point that they could export crisps and/or flavouring to far-off countries that had been begging for supplies for years.

BECOMING
A NATIONAL
INSTITUTION

TAYTO, TAYTO EVERYWHERE

From Hector Grey to Mattress Mick, Dublin has often found itself home to businesspeople with a remarkable talent for selling their goods in a quirky yet personable fashion. Joe Murphy was a prime example of this type, combining his niche-seeking ingenuity and ad lib engineering skills with his inherent flair for sales and publicity. His approach to marketing involved an assortment of playful, inter-active and philanthropic campaigns, from loud attention-grabbing spectacles to humble community outreach projects. This is part of the reason why Tayto so quickly became a part of the fabric of Irish society, and it's an approach that Tayto continues with to this day.

In 1956, Joe went down the attention-grabbing route when he com-missioned the Neon Electric Sign Company of Talbot Street to make and install a neon sign that no Dubliner could possibly avoid. For £70 per year, he rented a space along the side of the Lafayette Building, which stood in one of Dublin's busiest and most photo-graphed locations, towering over the south side of the O'Connell Bridge. The glowing sign spanned four of the building's six storeys and featured the company's name in vertical lettering, with a neon Mr Tayto perched in the top left corner (and a 'Fun Foods' later added along the bottom). Sitting alongside signs for Aer Lingus and Gold Flake cigarettes, it helped to establish the building as a landmark and meeting place, and gave Tayto an unmissable 24/7 brand presence for the next twenty-one years – until Dublin Corporation embarked upon a rampage of 'tidying up the visual aspect' of the city by refusing permission to such branding.

(**OPPOSITE**) The iconic Tayto neon sign, a constant presence – day and night – on the side of Dublin's Lafayette Building for over two decades. (Lafayette Photography)

(**LEFT**) (Dublin City Libraries)

Joe was also quick off the mark to realize the potential exposure offered by Dublin's famous St. Patrick's Day Parade. A number of companies participated in the 1956 parade, by sending along a float or a branded vehicle. Tayto made their presence known with six multicoloured vans featuring their logo, mascot and packets of crisps painted on all sides. An early practitioner of guerrilla marketing (an approach that wouldn't be identified and named for another thirty years), Joe would often arrange for one of his eye-catching vans to 'break down' on O'Connell Street during peak hours. Or if there was a big match on in Croke Park, he'd send out all six of his vans to drive around the area in circles all day – which would be spotted by tens of thousands of punters, on the way to and from the stadium. 'How many vans do you have?' someone once asked him. 'I was at the All-Ireland on Sunday and I must have seen dozens!' Of course, the sales team would have prepared for this stunt well in advance – by making sure that every pub and shop in the area had received multiples of their usual order in the days before the game.

RADIO TAYTO

Listen to the
"Cruise with Tayto"
Programme
EVERY SATURDAY MORNING
8.45 a.m. FROM RADIO EIREANN
Ask for Tayto Crisps
A flavour to suit every palate (also plain)
ON SALE EVERYWHERE
"Those who know buy Tayto"

Joe recognized the need for Tayto to establish good communication with its audience, and was one of the first entrepreneurs to sponsor a programme on Raidio Éireann. By December 1954, within six months of Tayto's launch, listeners could tune into the fifteen-minute *Cruise With Tayto* (also known as *Cruising With Tayto*) every Saturday morning from 8.45 am. This segment evolved into *The Tayto Programme*, which often invited listeners to send in a postcard in exchange for some freebies, like a free branded pencil sharpener or a tin of Tayto. By the late 50s, Tayto was sponsoring Harry Thuillier's *Leisure Time*, which saw the former fencer and prolific broadcaster inviting listeners to 'take it easy with Tayto to the sounds of easy-listening tunes'. Unsurprisingly, *Leisure Time* soon became better known as *The Tayto Show*. Every Tuesday afternoon, Thuillier had a segment called 'Guess the Mystery Personality', which involved a trio of panellists trying to guess who was on the other side of a curtain, through a series of probing 'yes' or 'no' questions. Frank Hall (of Hall's Pictorial Weekly) later reminisced about how he was roped into being the mystery personality one week, unaware of how seriously Thuillier and his crew treated this top secret game. Hall ended up spending a period of time in a backstage wardrobe with a potato sack over his head, feeling like the victim of a kidnapping, before being interrogated by three strangers. After all of that, the contestants were easily able to identify the celebrity satirist.

All of these radio spots got people talking – but none so much as the All-Ireland Tayto Quiz Championship. In his memoir, Memory Man, broadcasting legend Jimmy Magee takes credit for this idea. He claims that Thuillier instructed him to come up with a new segment idea to pitch to Joe the following morning. Fast forward to him sitting down at the meeting, mind still blank, when suddenly he started articulating an idea as it came to him. He pitched something called the 'Tayto Family Show', a quiz show that would tour across Ireland, recording in halls and clubs, usually as part of a variety night, before being aired on the radio on a Friday afternoon. The winning team would go on to represent their county in the All-Ireland of trivia. The concept was a hit, and the show took to the road. In 1963, Laois defeated Cavan in what one newspaper called 'a ding dong final'. They went on to represent Ireland in the Tayto International World Cup of Quiz, where they competed against other eggheads from England, Germany, Australia, Canada, Austria and the USA. Having won Ireland's first-ever World Cup, the hero quizzers returned home to Laois with a silver trophy and gold pencils.

In an extra twist to the format, Joe decided that one schoolchild from the winning county should receive a £1,600 university scholarship – £400 per year for any four-year course in Science, Engineering, Arts or Architecture. Sligo won 1964's quiz, so six secondary school students from around the county ended up pitting it out in a general knowledge quiz. In the end, Mary Shinnors from Ballisodare was presented with the scholarship by Joe Murphy, Harry Thuillier and the Minister for Education – and future Irish President – Patrick Hillery.

Joe's canny marketing methods meant that Tayto wasted no time in achieving a presence all over the country – even at Ireland's smallest and possibly most remote shop. Located in Donegal's spectacular Barnes Mountain Gap, this landmark and crucial pitstop was run by Mary Gallagher, better known as 'Mary The Gap'.

TAYTO BABY competition

1960—Seamus Reilly of Cavan.

1961—Catherine Wolverson of Dublin.

'A Handsome cheque will be presented to the mother of the first baby born in 1963. Write in, time of birth, to Baby Competition, Tayto Ltd., Rathmines, Dublin. 6.

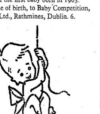

1962—Angela Treacher of Dublin.

who will be the 1963 TAYTO BABY?

TAYTO BABY OF THE YEAR

Another initiative that got the whole country involved was the Tayto Baby Competition. In late 1959, it was announced that 'a handsome cheque will be presented to the mother of the first baby born' in 1960. The inaugural Tayto Baby would prove to be Seamus Reilly, who timed his entrance perfectly. Bunny Murphy (Joe's wife) duly made her way to Cavan, to present to Seamus's mother a cheque worth £20. A couple of years later, Marcella Doyle of Ballyfermot would give birth just fourteen minutes into the new year and her daughter Sarah, unbeknownst to her, was officially crowned 'The 1963 Tayto Baby'. A newspaper headline the next day declared 'MOTHER GETS CHEQUE' and a Tayto spokesperson said that they were 'anxious to know if that time could be beaten'. The next year, a baby born at 00:08 was in the lead until Tayto got word that another baby all the way down in Kerry had been born three minutes earlier, so Freda Purcell's mother Sheila took the money instead. As if that wasn't enough, the 1968 Tayto Baby reared its head at just *four* minutes past midnight. Safe to say, it was a highly competitive and much sought-after title that had every Irish new-born-to-be clambering for a January 1st birthday.

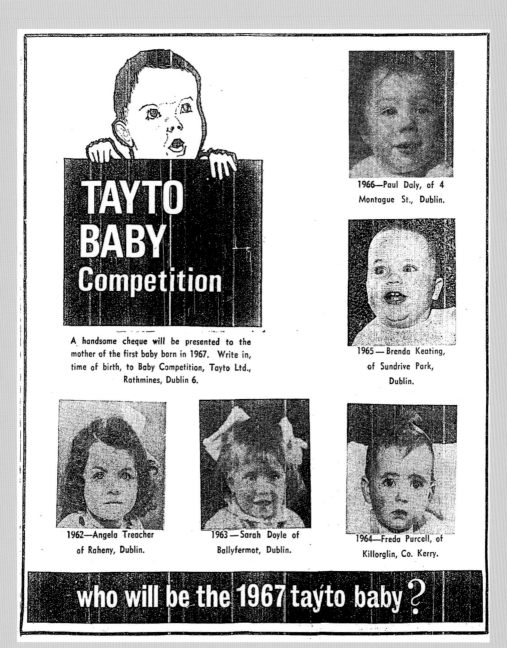

Notices such as these were posted in the newspapers towards the end of every year.
You'll notice that Tayto even ensured to use updated photos of former Tayto Babies.

Tayto's Kevin Masterson presenting a sponsorship cheque to the Meath-Tayto team of 1979: Jack Murphy, Kevin Reilly, Ben McKenna (manager), Eddie Connolly, Stephen Crotty and Gabriel Howard. They competed in that year's Rás Tailteann, which was eventually won by future Tour de France winner Stephen Roche. Tayto had been the first-ever sponsor of the Rás Tailteann, back in 1973.

THE TAYTO CUP(S)

Tayto didn't only encourage babies to compete. By the 1960s, people of all ages and disciplines were competing to win one of a number of Tayto-sponsored prizes at events across the country. There was a Tayto Cup for show jumping at the Kill O' The Grange races, a Tayto Cup for darts at the Carrick-on-Shannon Darts Championship, a Tayto Cup for golfing at Woodbrook Golf Club, and a Tayto Cup for waterskiing at the Irish Open Waterskiing Championships in Killaloe. In 1964, this waterskiing trophy was won by Sligo student Alan Murray, who managed to beat athletes from more likely skiing strongholds like France and Switzerland. During his victory lap, Murray treated onlookers to a bout of barefoot skiing, as he glided over Lough Derg at fifty miles per hour.

[...] there was a Tayto Cup for the highest-scoring potatoes. (In 1960, this one was – somewhat ironically – won by a 'W. Pringle'.)

Tayto Cups were not the sole preserve of sportspeople, either. There were Tayto Cups for juvenile bands at the Letterkenny Folk Festival and Mary From Dungloe Festival, a Tayto Cup for singing at Milltown Feis, and even a Tayto Cup for Terriers at the Churchtown Dog Show. There was a Tayto Challenge Trophy for youth dancers at Féile an Crócaige. At the Annual Show of the National Garden Association in Molesworth Hall, the Tayto Perpetual Cup was awarded to the person with the highest-scoring vegetables. At the Annual Show of the Kilternan and North-East Wicklow Young Farmers Clubs, there was a Tayto Cup for the highest-scoring potatoes. (In 1960, this one was – somewhat ironically – won by a 'W. Pringle'.) Tayto also sponsored a Potato Growing Competition for members of the youth organisation Macra na Tuaithe. Ten prizes of £5 each were awarded to whichever youngsters could grow the most impressive plots of potatoes. 'By the way,' the newspaper notice clarified, 'the bag of potatoes which you send to Dublin for adjudication WILL BE PAID FOR by Tayto, so you won't be out of pocket for that.' Tayto also sponsored what was – for its duration – the greatest honour in Irish theatre: the annual award presented by the Variety Artistes Trust Society. As well as a trophy, each winner was presented with a portrait of themselves – fully funded by Tayto.

Not only did these Tayto Cups help to foster community connections in every pocket and corner of the country, but Tayto also received great exposure at these events, as well as afterwards, when the results were reported in the media. Tayto was everywhere: on a sign being towed by a plane above the Tydavnet Parish Show in Monaghan, on posters around Kells for the Tayto Social Club, and at bicycle races around the country (Tayto being a sponsor of cyclist Eamonn Connolly, Dublin's Clann Brugha Cycling Club and the Meath team, better known as the 'Meath-Tayto team'). Tayto sponsored a Children's Potato Crisp Eating Competition at the Glenfarne Gala; pantomime performances for underprivileged children at the Walkinstown Apollo; the Irish Blind Chess Team's trip to the Blind Chess Olympiad in Yugoslavia; a pram race – for adult babies – at Kells Fáilte Week; and Dublin's famous Liffey Swim. In 1979, Tayto funded a £2,000 UCD soccer scholarship for a teenager looking to blend sport with an academic career. The brain-child of Dr Tony O'Neill, these scholarships were an attempt to coun-teract the drain of promising young players dropping out of school to go to English clubs on an 'apprenticeship' which would involve them cleaning boots and sweeping terraces – with only one in ten ever securing a senior contract across the water.

Tayto's presence could even be felt on the remote islands of Ireland in the dead of winter. When The Islands Relief Organisation arranged for supplies to be parachuted to 'the isolated island peoples', Tayto was one of the firms that 'contributed generously', alongside John Player and Sons, John Power and Sons and Urney Chocolates. After boxes of cigarettes, whiskey, sweets and crisps rained down on the islanders from the skies above, one can only imagine that there were a fair few knees-up across the isles that evening.

(TOP LEFT) Tayto execs (including financial controller Matt Duane and Vincent O'Sullivan) with TD Jim Tunney and a Community Games athlete representing County Monaghan.

(TOP MIDDLE) Kevin Masterson (front right, holding the dartboard) with Smith's Darts Team, inaugural champions of the Carrick-on Shannon Darts Championship Cup in 1964.

(TOP RIGHT) Some winners at the 1985 Community Games.

(CENTRE LEFT) The 1965 Tayto Cup being presented to 'The Good Companions' darts team.

(CENTRE MIDDLE) The Meath-Tayto cycling team of 1978, who were the winning County Team at that year's Rás Tailteann.

(CENTRE RIGHT) The 1965 Tayto Cup being presented to Old Christians GAA club in Limerick.

(BOTTOM RIGHT) Kevin Masterson (far left) with Ben Kealy (second from right) and other Tayto execs, pictured with members of Ireland's 1968 swim team. At that summer's Mexico Olympics, they became the first Irish Olympian swimmers since 1928.

THE COMMUNITY GAMES

There was yet *another* Tayto Cup, known to children and teenagers all over the land. Along with around 1,000 medals, this one was presented to the winners at the national finals of the Community Games. The Games were hosted annually at Butlin's holiday centre in the seaside village of Mosney in County Meath. Every summer, thousands of children decamped to – and camped *in* – Mosney, to compete in everything from table tennis and rounders to model making and chess. Inspired by the Mexico City Olympics, the Games had been founded by Joe Connolly in Walkinstown in 1967, in an effort to promote grassroots sports and community participation. These were two things that a certain snack company simply couldn't resist, and Tayto became heavily involved as a sponsor in the late 70s – a partnership that lasted twelve years. Spud's son Barry theorized that his dad was such

an advocate of events like these because Joe – like many city kids – had grown up without a garden or even a whole lot of local green space. Meanwhile, Barry and his siblings were being raised in a home with a number of luxurious mod cons, including a tennis court and swimming pool. Joe loved the idea of any initiative that gave children access to otherwise inaccessible facilities, a place to stretch their legs and the social even of the summer, every summer. 'He was just a proud Dub', according to his son Stephen, 'who knew that he was very lucky' – so sponsoring events like the Community Games was 'his way of giving back.' Joe was also a keen sportsman himself, with a special passion for waterskiing, tennis and – especially later in life – golf. A photograph even exists, but sadly cannot be found, of Joe waterskiing while smoking a pipe and reading an upside-down newspaper.

MR TAYTO AND MR PLATO

When the Coolock factory opened and the majority of production was moved there, it freed up one of the four buildings at Tayto's Rathmines location (the other three were still in use, primarily making popcorn). Joe quietly established a side enterprise that he dubbed 'Sign Sell', and recruited his trusty sign-writer/screen-printer Mick Jones to take charge of operations. Joe Jr even took a summer job working there one year, and the younger Murphy children would occasionally pitch in, too. Over the next year or so, Sign Sell was used as a base to print up all kinds of Tayto branding and merchandise, from pens and rulers to point-of-sale material and Tayto banners for grocers to hang outside their shops. Joe even assembled his kids into a sort of 'street team', sending them into school with branded stationery to distribute to their fellow pupils.

In 1964, upon realizing that every pub in the country had an ashtray on each of its tables (and an array of Tayto snacks behind the bar), the Tayto team got to work printing Mr Tayto on to a batch of ashtrays, and then dispatching to hundreds of publicans. They also sent some out to members of the press, including one columnist at *The Irish Times* who deemed it to be 'the weirdest propaganda of the week' on Valentine's Day of that year.

In another pub-centric promotion, from 1959, Tayto challenged the public to find 'The Tayto Man'. This wasn't as easy as just spotting somebody in a big, obvious Mr Tayto costume. *This* Tayto Man was just

At one stage, Tayto also created a series of beer mats with humorous cartoons, known as 'Tayto Quips', printed upon them.

an ordinary-looking fellow whose only identifying feature was that he'd have a newspaper under his arm. Through the press, punters would be told a general area and time to look for him. Whoever spotted the enigmatic figure was instructed to hold out a packet of Tayto and declare 'You're the Tayto man!' If correct, the lucky winner would earn themselves a guinea – enough for a feed of three pints and fourteen bags of Tayto.

A 1973 promotion saw Tayto offering customers a free gramophone ... sort of. After sending away a certain number of empty Tayto packets, you would receive several pieces of cardboard in return. After assembling it into the general shape of a record player, you placed a plastic disc on the turntable and twirled the record around, with your finger acting as the needle, to create sound. For your efforts, you'd be rewarded with the scratchy, tinny voice of comedian and actor Frank Kelly reciting a poetic verse, as heard on the radio:

Tayto's cutting edge 'DISCOTAYTO' gramophone.

Long ago, that wise
Greek, Mr Plato,
Made a forecast
about the potato.
'I can see that one day,
They'll be sliced,'
he would say.
'Deep fried until crisp,
And called "Tayto".'

During the summer of 1970, lucky Tayto-munchers went undercover as trenchcoat-wearing gumshoes in an effort to win prizes like Moon Globes (after the previous year's lunar landing, interest in the Moon was at an all-time high) and Rotadraw kits (rotating stencils that budding artists could use to draw mystery pictures).

Staff at Tayto HQ going through some of the entries for the World Cup competition during the summer of 1978. To coincide with the tournament in Argentina, Tayto offered customers the chance to win one of 25 televisions, 100 portable radios and 100 footballs.

According to one eco-conscious winner, 'What really pleased me was the fact that one had to send in eight empty bags (as well as a suitable slogan), and all eight had been picked up by me off the streets of the town!'

Additional gramophone discs could be obtained by sending away four empty packets, along with a fourpenny stamp. Incidentally, Frank Kelly would go on to play Fr Jack in the sitcom *Father Ted*, where – at one point – Fr Ted asks his hopeless colleague Fr Dougal, 'How did you get into the Church? Was it like, "Collect twelve crisp packets and become a priest?"'

Always one to embrace progress, Tayto ran the 'Surf the Net for Free' competition in 1996, during the early days of the Internet, with the top prize going to the school group that could design the best Tayto website. The national winners were Mr O'Neachtain's Third Class from Edmund Rice Primary School in Tramore. Having heard about the competition, they quickly figured out what exactly a 'website' was, and then – with a little bit of help from the older boys at the neighbouring secondary school – put together a charming little site with drawings, puzzles, games, Tayto recipe ideas and even some fan fiction about Mr Tayto and his supposed wife and kids ('I was lucky that I wasn't turned into a crisp, but was selected to be their mascot and logo,' Mr Tayto writes in their own unique version of Tayto history). To reward the class for their cyber skills and creativity, Mr Tayto travelled down to Waterford to present all twenty-six boys in the class with a Sony PlayStation and a game each – as well as a top-of-the-range computer and a year's free internet access for their school.

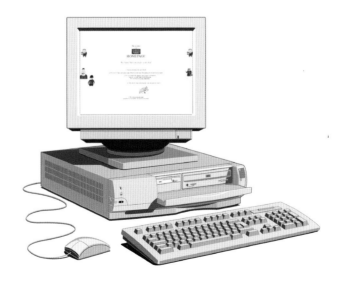

TAYTO AT THE RDS

During the 20th century, the Ballsbridge headquarters of the Royal Dublin Society played host to a number of annual events and conventions – usually dedicated to the advancement of Irish agriculture and equestrianism. Amongst them were the Spring Show (dating back to 1831) and the National Horse Show (1864), which both – over time – evolved into two of the largest events on the Irish agricultural calendar. The Spring Show featured prize-givings, exhibitions and lectures, whereas the Horse Show's primary focus is on equestrian displays and competitions.

Both jamborees *also* welcomed a concurrent trade fair in the vast expanse of the RDS's halls and arenas, to showcase the best of domestic food, drink and industry. Unsuprisingly, Tayto was a familiar presence at these fairs and would attend each year with a different eye-catching stall, lavishly illustrated with its products, logos and mascots. In August 1959, they had one of 238 trade stands at the Horse Show, setting up shop in the Serpentine Hall alongside all of the titans of Irish industry, including Guinness, Aer Lingus and The Dublin Shirt and Collar Company.

TEN LUCKY PEOPLE

have a special surprise waiting for them when they visit Stand No. 219 in the Serpentine Hall at the Spring Show this week! YOU may be one of the ten! It's well worth your while making sure of your chance by visiting the TAYTO Stand!

(OPPOSITE) An example of one of Tayto's eye-catching stands in the RDS, this one being from the mid 80s.

(LEFT) A small ad from May 1960, as discreet and cryptic as any secret spy communication – or perhaps one of Willy Wonka's marketing techniques. Whatever 'surprise' these invitees received, it should be noted that *Charlie and the Chocolate Factory* wouldn't be published for another four years!

TAYTO POPCORN: NOT FOR HORSES

Tayto proving to be
a hit with the kids at
the RDS in 1980.

With tens of thousands in attendance – including household names and decision-makers – the RDS was an unmissable opportunity for Tayto to meet the public, promote new products, gain some column inches, and network with farmers and other businesses. It also offered an excuse for Joe to raise some funds for causes close to his heart. Each year, the proceeds from stock sold at the fairs would be donated to a needy beneficiary. Joe was especially fond of the Central Remedial Clinic, a Dublin charity for people with disabilities, helping to fundraise for them on many occasions.

In the early 60s came the launch of Tayto Popcorn for twopence a bag – half the price of the crisps. To gauge how customers felt about their recipe, the sales team brought free samples to branches of Powers' Supermarkets. As part of this roadshow, they also brought their popcorn maker along to the Horse Show. The intention was to introduce their new product to consumers from outside of Dublin, and to supply punters with delicious fresh batches of the snack. In a lapse of judgement, however, the Tayto gang was given a stall next to the show-jumping parade ring. When the horses heard the popping of the kernels, they freaked out, mistaking the noise for something more sinister – perhaps thinking that they were after clip-clopping into a Western film. So startled were they that Tayto was forced to abandon the promotion, and back to Powers' Supermarkets with the popcorn they went!

Although the last ever Spring Show was held in 1992, the Horse Show is still a massive date on the equestrian calendar – and Tayto still has an occasional presence there, with Mr Tayto having now replaced singers, sports stars and politicians as the ultimate celeb sighting for horse lovers of all ages.

Stands you should visit

Known throughout the length and breadth of Ireland is the name TAYTO. Our picture shows Mr. H. Murray, sales manager, and Miss Louise Radner. On display are the famed products: Tayto Pack; Pete's Peanuts and the ever popular Tayto Crisps. —Advt.

THE
COOLOCK
ERA

An early pack of Tayto, bearing the price of a florin (two shillings).

A CALL FROM CHICAGO

In 1964, Tayto came to the attention of the major Chicago-based conglomerate Beatrice Foods. Founded in the small Nebraska town of Beatrice in 1894, Beatrice Foods had grown from a local creamery into the fifth-largest food company in the USA and was actively looking to expand its food operations. This era saw them acquire a number of tasty firms – manufacturers of candy bars, cookies, pickles, sweets, olives and cherries – across the world. Meanwhile, President John F. Kennedy's visit to Ireland in June 1963 had helped to shine a spotlight on our island, strengthening Irish-American ties in the process.

The president of Beatrice, William G. Karnes, was of Irish descent and first had his curiosity piqued after spotting a Tayto-centric article in a trade journal. The article made note of Tayto's ventures on to the radio airwaves, where they had given a scholarship to one lucky listener. More accustomed to companies using their own stock as cheap competition prizes, Karnes was struck by the ingenuity of a company engaging in such unorthodox brand exposure. He sent Joseph H. Rogatnick – his Director of European Development – to visit Joe, who reported back to him favourably. Karnes promptly invited Joe to Chicago for a chat.

'Joe,' he supposedly said at their meeting, 'our people tell me your equipment is shoddy and your plant is falling apart. Let's say our fellows went into your plant and beat up everything there with sledgehammers; it wouldn't affect our offer at all. The only things we're really buying from you are five letters: T, A, Y, T, O.' Perhaps for dramatic effect, he was neglecting to reference two other key factors to Tayto's success: the secret recipe, and Joe's talented workforce.

Joe was reluctant to sell. It wasn't the first time that he'd been approached with an offer. Just a few years prior, he'd rebuffed the advances of Smith's Crisps, the English company that – in the 1920s – had invented the concept of plain crisps being packaged with a twist of salt. This time, however, Joe recognized the need for a partner with the money and resources to help Tayto to achieve its full potential.

The autostereogram automobile: Joe receiving delivery of his new 3-D truck from Mr Callow of Callow Motor Mechanics on Westland Row. (O'Malley Pictures Ltd.)

Beatrice – with its 25,000 employees producing over 5,000 products across twenty-three countries – seemed like an ideal match. Karnes negotiated to purchase a 75 per cent stake in Tayto, leaving Joe with a quarter of the company, on one condition: that it would remain autonomous and wouldn't be taking orders from a Chicago skyscraper.

> 'I sold because the banks were putting the squeeze on me. I had, like many other businesses, an overdraft and the bank wanted its money back. Not only could I not afford to pay them back because I was expanding my business, but I wanted even more money to expand it further. There was no way I could get more money. And now, years later, it makes me vomit whenever I see that any renegade roughneck, it would appear, can walk into a bank, put a basket on the counter and ask for a half a million pounds, saying "Here's my fountain pen for security." If the banks gave attention to the Joe Murphys, then you'd have a much better country today.' – Joe Murphy

The £250,000 deal was announced publicly on October 22nd. In one fell swoop, Joe – just forty years of age – had become one of Ireland's first self-made millionaires of the post-war era. When asked by a reporter if he was now extremely rich, he understatedly replied, 'You could describe me as a *dollar* millionaire.' When he got back to Dublin, he went into the bank that held the deeds of his house – Annacreevy on Adelaide Road, Glenageary – and cleared what was left of his £3,500 mortgage. He then returned to his debt-free home with a new mink coat for Bunny, and soon afterwards bought himself a brand new white Rolls-Royce, complete with tinted windows. He would become known for his Rolls-Royces, at a time when there were only a few dozen of them in the country, and upgraded to the latest model every second year. Valets would scramble to park it, knowing that a tip from Joe would likely double their week's wage. Children would sprint to surround his car, too – but not to admire the high-class vehicle. 'Mr Murphy, Mr Murphy, have you any crisps?' they'd holler. Once, with no crisps on board, he instead offered them gold-plated pens

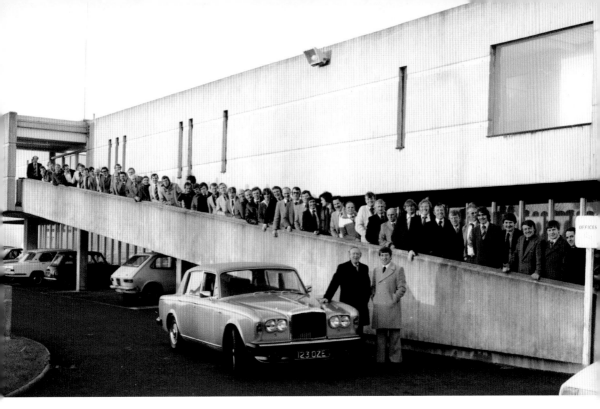

One of Joe's Rolls-Royces took centre stage for this photograph of Tayto management outside the Coolock factory. (Lensmen)

with 'Tayto' engraved on the side. Alas, the kids had no interest in fancy pens; for them, it was crisps or nothing.

At the time of the Beatrice sale, Joe told the press that he now had plans for the erection of a new factory on a three-acre site. Meanwhile, he'd be staying on as Managing Director (on a salary of £8,000 per year) and would be looking to double his 120-person workforce 'in a very short time.'

> 'There were a number of other reasons why we wanted to purchase a majority interest in Tayto. The most decisive one was Murphy. He was different. What impressed us the most was his awareness of the importance of sound marketing, with emphasis on value and quality. He was a doer, a goer and a winner. He was convinced that with a new plant and additional working capital, the potential for Tayto was unlimited.' – William G. Karnes

COOLOCK

The main incentive of the Beatrice deal was that it allowed Tayto access to the capital required to build a brand new plant – somewhere with the technology and capacity to sustain Tayto well into the future. Up until this point, Tayto hadn't strayed far from Dublin's elliptical city limits, as defined by the Royal and Grand Canals. But having long outgrown rented rooms in the city and warehouses wedged down urban laneways, they badly required a campus of their own. At that time, the hope was for a factory large enough to potentially allow them to begin production of a larger range of snack foods – including Korn Kurls, Caramel Corn, Snack Chips, Bacon Rinds, and other products created by the Adams Corporation, another subsidiary of Beatrice Foods. Joe looked about ten kilometres north of his current premises, to the small village of Coolock.

Back then, Coolock was at the very edge of suburban Dublin, and a convenient distance from the farms of north county Dublin from where Tayto sourced their potatoes. Having previously been farmland itself, Coolock was witnessing rapid development and had undergone a 92 per cent population increase during the first five years of the 60s. This was due to Dublin Corporation overseeing a large-scale slum clearance, moving people from cramped inner-city tenements to local authority houses in the new suburbs. The Dublin Corporation Housing Committee – chaired by Jim Larkin's son, Denis – sold Tayto a three-acre corner site for £6,900, plus an additional rent of £600 per year. Joe used his entrepreneurial flair to attract special tax incentives and a government grant amounting to around 40 per cent of the cost of the development. Having just transplanted huge masses of people into the area, the powers-that-be were now keen to entice companies that could provide employment for the new locals.

And so, in July 1966, Tayto applied for planning permission 'to erect a potato crisp plant on the site at the junction of Greencastle and Malahide Roads'. Once planning was approved, architect –

On the 10th of September 1968, the £500,000 factory was officially opened by George Colley, the Minister for Industry and Commerce – pictured here alongside Joe Murphy, Allan Wilfred Adams (co-founder of Adams Corporation of Beloit, Wisconsin, who had invented the cheese puff before being bought by Beatrice in 1960) and Seán Lemass (who had recently stepped down as Taoiseach, but was still a serving TD). (Lensmen)

and author of *Town Planning in Ireland* – David Cronin got to work, with practical input from Egon Bohn, Beatrice Food's chief engineer. It was determined that the 40,000-square-foot new building would consist of four main areas:

- **Potato storage:** a 10,000-square-foot environmentally controlled space, containing a temporary sack storage area, three conditioning bins and a bulk store.
- **Production:** a state-of-the-art 17,250-square-foot space, where potatoes would be processed, sliced, cooked, weighed, bagged and sealed.
- **Administrative space:** offices located on the first floor, with windows overlooking the production area.
- **Staff facilities:** personnel welfare accommodation, comprising a spacious smoking lounge, canteen, dining room, cloakroom and toilets.

On the 1st of May 1968, the spiral elevators and conveyor belts of Europe's most modern crisp factory were switched on for the first time, and plumes of smoke started piping from its chimneys. More than 120 employees and their families turned out to witness the occasion – and to help produce around 250 boxes of crisps during this first day warm-up session. After discussions and trials with packaging company Jefferson Smurfit, Tayto had just introduced the cardboard carton as their method of choice for transporting crisps. Each box could contain thirty-six packets, which was a vast improvement on previous systems. Potato crisp production would be entirely moved to the new plant, while the Rathmines and Harold's Cross facilities shifted their focus to peanuts and popcorn. In Rathmines, the production of butterscotch-flavoured popcorn – based on a recipe from Beatrice – had just begun. Although this was intended for the export market, it led to some experimentation with other sweet recipes, which resulted in the launch of a Toffee Popcorn and a pink-and-yellow candy popcorn called Totem Popcorn. At this point, the full range of snacks began to be referred to – and marketed as – 'Tayto Fun Foods'.

The new factory was just across the Greencastle Road from Cadbury, who had moved there in 1964. Locals from the time that both factories co-existed still talk about this industrial intersection as though it were some magical place from a children's fantasy book, and remember high levels of curiosity as to what went on inside these big mysterious buildings. A whole generation of Northsiders also remember the tantalizing smells. Depending on the wind direction, there'd be an overpowering aroma of melting chocolate or freshly fried crisps – and sometimes both at once. It could be theorized that this coincidental combination is what led some Dubliners to have a unique propensity for eating milk chocolate and Cheese & Onion Tayto in the same mouthful – a combo that Tayto would eventually experiment with, several decades later. In the 70s, another factory – Chivers jam factory – opened next door to the chocolate factory, further contributing to the area's alluring smorgasbord of nasal treats.

Inside the Tayto factory, the new setup was capable of producing close to a thousand bags of crisps per minute. Thinking back to his earlier factories, where 'each girl had her own little cooker' and Bernie Kane hand-sealed every bag with a paintbrush and glue, Joe proudly pointed out that 'Now we have fourteen high-speed packing machines on the factory floor, and each one can seal seventy bags per minute.' Flicking through his well-thumbed copy of A. E. Williams's *Potato Crisps* manual, he said, 'There are some weird machines illustrated here. I can show you machines downstairs which have an output 500 times the output of these. See those old slicers? They used to take one potato at a time.' Then, pointing to a high-tech (for 1951) slicer, he joked, 'This one was an advanced model, which took four potatoes – but a girl needed to have four hands to operate it efficiently.'

TAYTO GROUP COMPANIES

EUROSNAX INTERNATIONAL LTD.,
MOUNT TALLANT AVE., TERENURE,
DUBLIN 6. TELEPHONE 904691 (5 lines)
964020

KING FOODS LTD.,
JAMESTOWN RD., INCHICORE,
DUBLIN 8. TELEPHONE 266495/265683.
TELEX 30787

SUBSIDIARY OF Beatrice Foods Co. U.S.A.

(ABOVE) After more than a decade trying to keep up with public demand, Joe finally got to open the huge, custom-designed factory that would become his playground.

(BELOW) Joe Murphy pictured at a function in the 90s alongside Tayto's first-ever employee, Bernie Kane. Bernie was hired in 1954 and stayed with Tayto for the rest of her career. 'It was a huge part of her life,' said one close friend, after Bernie passed away in August 2024. 'She was the backbone of the factory,' according to Barry Murphy, 'keeping all the girls going on the production line.'

After reading aloud a line from the book – 'The flow of gum is controlled by a cock, located immediately above the brass wheel' – Joe excitedly interrupted himself. 'My God!' he exclaimed. 'It seems incredible today. It's like as if Alcock and Brown came back and were suddenly put aboard the Concorde!'

Tayto soon had over 300 employees across its various factories – but, as Joe pointed out, 'We employ more people outside the factory than inside.' Of his hundreds of employees, the first person who Joe greeted every day was Paddy Enright, who had what was known as 'the dirtiest job in the factory'. Paddy worked in a pit, receiving all of the spud deliveries and then loading them on to a flume into the factory. A firm believer in the importance of maintaining contact – and a feedback loop – with his customers, Joe still largely eschewed wholesalers, and instead had a fleet of 100 trucks and 11 distribution depots nationwide.

Tayto Limited

Packers of Savoury Specialities
Greencastle Road Coolock
Dublin 5 Ireland

(ABOVE) The company postmark, stamped on an envelope from the 70s.

(OPPOSITE) Workers on the Coolock factory floor ensuring that only the best Tayto make it into the packet.

Over the years, Tayto had become accustomed to being short on stock and battling to keep up with demand – so much so that it had been assumed their produce would continue to be sent off to depots the moment that it had been bagged and boxed. Due to this naivety, one thing that the new plant lacked was a warehouse facility. In no time at all, production had increased to the point that storage suddenly became a problem, for the first time ever, and boxes of crisps were piling up in every nook, cranny, corridor and office in the building. Just a week after the factory's official launch, work commenced on a huge warehouse extension to the side, which was completed in 1969. It was a good thing that they started building as soon as they had, because 1969 was a year that Tayto produced seventy million packets of potato crisps and fifteen million packets of other snacks – more than doubling their annual output since the beginning of the decade.

> Job creation is not half as important as the creation of productive jobs. – Joe Murphy

The new factory also gave Tayto the capacity to start expanding their flavour range.

As well as crisp storage, 1968 also saw Tayto needing to open its first *potato* storage facility. For the past few years, Tayto had been contracting Meath farmers for a guaranteed supply of potatoes – always stressing in their call-outs that quality was their main concern and that the price was 'a secondary considera-tion'. It therefore made sense to build a storage unit in Stamullen, close to where many of their potatoes were now being grown. This new repository had the capacity to store around 8,000 tonnes of potatoes – just over a year's supply for the company at that point. Because it was environmentally controlled, Tayto could finally start stockpiling and planning ahead without forever being at the mercy of the erratic Irish weather.

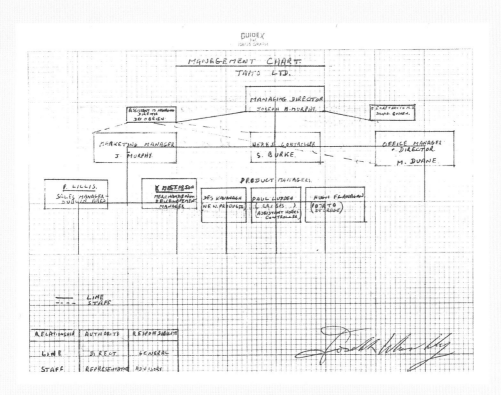

Tayto's company structure as of 1968, charted by Seamus Burke and signed by Joe Murphy.

A Tayto employee engaging in a spot of quality control.

COMPETITION

Sales grew exponentially during the 1960s, despite a number of new competitors who had been spurred on by Tayto's success. In 1961, after Joe had declined their takeover bid, Smith's set up their own plant next to the Clarnico-Murray sweet factory on Mount Tallant Avenue in Terenure – and just up the road from Tayto's building in Harold's Cross. However, the English company struggled to compete with Tayto and in 1966, they sold the controlling interest of the company to W. & R. Jacob. Jacob's, who were in some senses the Tayto of the biscuit market, used its might – as well as a hugely popular 'The Man from U.N.C.L.E.' promotion – to significantly increase Smith's share of the market in the next couple of years.

Two other new crisp companies – King and Perri – came along in 1963. King Foods was founded by brothers Michael and Eugene Collins, based out of Ceebee's chipper on Parnell Street, before opening a factory on the Jamestown Road in Inchicore. Perri Crisps was founded by the Capaldis, an Irish-Italian family who also made Palm Grove ice cream in their factory on Santry's Shanowen Road. To give themselves *any* chance of competing with Tayto, Perri priced their crisps at threepence a bag – one penny less than Tayto. In their ads at the time, Tayto made sure to emphasize the quality and reputation of their product, and to remind people why The Original Irish Crisp was easily worth an extra penny.

For Tayto, there was never any reason to worry. As one child of that era puts it, 'We used to call them "Perri Tayto" because we thought that's what crisps were called.' Just like Hoover, Biro and Sellotape, Tayto had already attained synonymity – that holy grail of brand recognition, when a company name becomes a common noun by creating the defining version of a product.

In 1972, Tayto bought King Foods as part of its continued expansion. The Collins brothers stayed on at the company during a two-year transitionary period, as Joe developed separate marketing strategies for both of his brands – as well as introducing a range of King snacks including Chickatees, King Kong and French Fries. That same year, Perri was issued a High Court injunction to restrain them from 'packaging or selling its potato crisps in packets or containers resembling the red, white and blue colouring and format of the Tayto crisp package'. Joe had spotted that Perri had started using similarly coloured cellophane bags, which came packaged in a very similar carton to his – and he believed 'that the package now being used by Perri was calculated to confuse a purchaser into thinking that he or she was buying Tayto crisps and not Perri crisps'. To further irk Joe, Perri's mascot – Mr Perri – had just been given a makeover and was now sporting a yellow face and red trousers, just like Mr Tayto. Joe believed that Perri were 'trying to take an unfair and unlawful advantage' of 'a clear psychological association' that had been established between Tayto's branding and product. The judge agreed, and the Perri designers went back to the drawing board. This wasn't to be Joe's last struggle with the world of intellectual property. The following October, he expressed his frustration over the length of time it took to register a trademark in Ireland, where applicants would have to wait up to two years to find out if their mark is registrable. 'The prospect of this inevitable time lag has often caused me to abandon registering a new trade name,' said Joe. 'To my knowledge, this complaint is shared by the majority of Irish manufacturers.'

Pub Crisps and classic Cheese & Onion being packaged at the Coolock factory.

By the end of the decade, a struggling Smith's Crisps had changed hands several more times, from Jacob's to Fitzwilton to Coca-Cola. According to one newspaper report, 'the Smith's potato crisp operation here is believed to have been running at a loss for many years, and the choice may well be to increase investment or to close down altogether'. In December 1980, more than two decades after Smith's tried to buy out Tayto, Tayto put in a reverse bid for the Irish operation of Smith's and its factory in Terenure. This takeover – approved by the Department of Industry, Commerce and Tourism – saved ninety-five jobs, bringing Tayto's total workforce to 475 (including 350 in Coolock). Popcorn and peanut production was moved to Inchicore, while Tayto rebranded the Mount Tallant factory as Eurosnax International, to be used for the production of snack products. In the 80s, all three Tayto factories would receive delivery of new packing machines – costing around £350,000 each – from Kliklok International. These machines ensured that the weight of each bag of crisps was within 0.5 per cent of its target weight.

THE CHANGING OF THE GUARD

In March 1981, at the age of fifty-seven, Joe decided to take a step back from the business – to enjoy an early semi-retirement in Spain – and was appointed to the position of 'Executive/Chairman'.

Stepping into the big shoes that Joe had worn since the very beginning, accountant Vincent O'Sullivan – who had spent three years as Financial Controller and seven years as Operations Manager – became Tayto's Managing Director for the next two decades. 'The main theme of this company is quality,' he said. 'Quality of produce and quality of service. We try to make a top-quality potato crisp for a low price. That's the main platform on which we were founded and that's the main one on which we'll continue.'

9th of March 1981: Joe Murphy, Ray Burke (Minister for the Environment) and Vincent O'Sullivan (Tayto's new MD) at the turning of the sod for the new storage plant in Balbriggan. 'Tayto is a good example of what the Irish entrepreneur is capable of achieving,' said Burke. Once complete, this six-acre development had the capacity to keep over 3,000 tonnes of spuds in perfect condition. (Lensmen)

BACK ON THE MARKET

Beatrice Foods had expanded rapidly since its acquisition of Tayto in 1964, and was a regular fixture in the top fifty of *Fortune Magazine's* annual 'Fortune 500' list. All manner of brands – from Tropicana to Krispy Kreme – were now under the Beatrice umbrella. However, the company ended up taking on too much debt after buying the holding company Esmark Inc. in the mid 80s. In 1987, Baltimore businessman Reginald Lewis bought Beatrice, and Tayto became part of a new company called TLC Beatrice International Holdings Inc. This purchase made Lewis the first African-American person to own a billion-dollar company. After his death in 1994, Lewis' wife Loida became the CEO of the company. In January 1997, she – along with Dublin's Lord Mayor Brendan Lynch – cut the ribbon on a new 30,000 square-foot central distribution centre in Ballymount, Dublin 12. With ten automated loading bays and the capacity to hold over 150,000 cartons of crisps, this facility helped to consolidate Tayto's distribution network of ten depots and thirty-five vans – ensuring that Tayto could guarantee fresh produce through weekly service calls to every outlet in Ireland.

In the late 90s, Lewis decided to wind down TLC Beatrice's European operations, and all of its constituent businesses went under the hammer. In a bid to take over the company, Tayto's managing director Vincent O'Sullivan teamed up with financial director Des Watchorn and senior executive Kevin Masterson, with Merrill Lynch as their investment banker. After PepsiCo/Walker's pulled out of the race, Vincent & co. were clear favourites to win the auction, and Lewis was hopeful that they would. However, to ensure that the bidding process remained impartial, she established a 'Chinese wall' (a barrier designed to prevent conflicts of interest within a company). In the end, Vincent was outbid by a few hundred grand, and in June 1999, Tayto was sold to drinks company Cantrell & Cochrane (C&C). In Loida's memoir, *Why Should Guys Have All the Fun?*, she writes about this moment, remembering that 'Both Vincent and I are crushed.'

Joe puts pen to paper during a Tayto boardroom meeting in the early 80s.

C&C

After thirty-five years of American ownership, the deeds to Tayto came home to Ireland, becoming a part of the portfolio of C&C – the makers of 'Club' soft drinks, Cidona and Bulmer's cider. 'We're absolutely happy to have the management on board with us to run the company,' said C&C's managing director Tony O'Brien. 'Any demotivation is likely to be short-lived, then it will be back to the reality of running the business for different owners.' Just a few months later, Vincent confirmed this sentiment, saying 'We have a very full and constructive relationship with C&C and the benefits of that relationship are already beginning to work through.' O'Brien believed that the pairing made perfect sense because 'the people who buy soft drinks also buy snack foods'. Amongst C&C's first moves were spending more than €4 million on a new production line for the Terenure factory, increasing the digitization of the company, recruiting additional personnel across all departments, and closing down the Inchicore factory.

Meanwhile, Loida Lewis – who described Tayto as 'the jewel in the Beatrice crown' – gifted one million dollars to employees of Tayto, as a gesture of appreciation for their work over the years (and after some discussions with the workers' unions). The bonuses averaged around €2,500 per employee, varying in size depending on their length of service. 'Mrs Lewis felt very strongly about this,' according to her spokesperson. 'She visited Dublin a number of times and got to know the people in Tayto. It's with mixed feelings that she is letting it go.' Indeed, Tayto's workforce was – according to Vincent O'Sullivan – 'rather like a family' and he highlighted the fact that 'the innovation of generations of people and their commitment to the company has been tremendous. Our people enjoy the work and they tend to stay with us.' After three decades at Tayto, he himself would say, 'I thought that it would be good experience for a few years, but it's turned out to be far more than that.'

The dawn of the new millennium was mired in challenges for the company and its new ownership. PepsiCo introduced Ireland to their Walker's brand on St Patrick's Day 2000, along with a series of high-profile ads starring a number of soccer and GAA stars. Tayto briefly lost some of its market share, although this was quickly rectified by its 2002 rebrand. 'We had a turbulent year in the Tayto business,' explained Tony O'Brien. 'In the middle of upgrading our manufacturing facilities, we ran into a lot of problems'.

THE END OF AN ERA

On the 28th of September 2001, Joe Murphy passed away in his sleep after a short battle with skin cancer, surrounded by his wife Bunny and children Yvonne, Joe, Barry, Peter and Stephen. Friends and acquaintances flocked to Iglesia El Angel in Marbella to pay their final respects to a pioneering entrepreneur and distinguished personality. The *Sunday Independent* hailed 'one of the best-known – and best-heeled – businessmen in the country', the *Belfast Telegraph* deemed him 'a major contributor to modern culture', and *The Irish Times* remembered 'a bon viveur... renowned for his humour and showmanship'.

Doting grandfather Joe with two of his grandchildren, Sarah and Stephen.

ENTER RAYMOND COYLE

In March 2003, a C&C spokesperson said that there had been a build-up of stock levels at the Coolock plant – a problem that they were going to solve by closing down the factory for a week, in what was an unprecedented first for the company. A few months later, they announced plans to close down the Terenure factory, reduce its workforce in Coolock and outsource production of snacks to Raymond Coyle's Largo Foods. 'The big issue is the fact that the entire market is facing a slowdown in the rate of growth,' according to the spokesperson. 'This is a short-term measure to address that.' Alas, this was still not enough. It was deemed that the Coolock HQ was in need of modernization – to the tune of €13.5 million – to ensure that Tayto remained the market leader. Instead, during the summer of 2005, C&C announced that the Coolock plant would be closed down – after nearly four decades in operation – and that all production would be contracted out to Largo.

Just a year later, C&C decided to sell Tayto to Largo Foods outright – a transaction that had been rumoured in the press, but denied by C&C, since the initial outsourcing in 2003. One of the losing bidders, Michael Carey of Jacob Fruitfield, later joked about how his bids had helped to drive up the auction price. Carey, an old friend of Coyle's, remembers that Ray 'phoned me two weeks later and said "You cost me €5 million." I apologised and he invited myself and my wife to dinner in his home.' Maurice Pratt, CEO of C&C, said, 'The price achieved for Tayto recognizes the value of its iconic brand position in the Irish market.' 'Tayto is the number-one brand in Ireland,' said Coyle, explaining his decision. 'Everybody knows it, and we knew the business – we were making the stuff. If we didn't get to buy it, more than likely we would have lost the co-packing arrangement.'

MR TAYTO

Mr Tayto poses alongside Pat Kenny outside Blackrock's Frascati Shopping Centre in this photo from 1996. This version of Mr Tayto marked the first time that he officially stepped off the crisp packet and into the real world. The year of his physical debut saw him travelling around the country presenting prizes and opening businesses – like one Carlow supermarket, which offered customers 'a chance to meet the funny Tayto Man'. (Lensmen)

THE POTATO MAN COMETH

Everybody's heard of a jacket potato – but who's ever heard of a potato in a jacket? Nobody, it seems – until October 1955, when Tayto's beloved mascot reared his head for the first time, tucked away in the corner of a newspaper advertisement.

This seminal illustration was drawn by Terry Myler, the daughter of painter Seán O'Sullivan and later a prolific cover artist of children's novels by the likes of Carolyn Swift and Peter Regan. Myler attended the National College of Art and Design on Kildare Street from the age of fourteen, before leaving to work for Arks advertising agency at sixteen. Seven years into the job, Myler says that she was handed a peeled potato and asked, 'Can you do something to make this look alive?' The evolution of Mr Tayto would become a collaborative effort over the next few years, with van-painter Leo Darbey and cartoonist Fred Thompson amongst a slew of artists to add their stamp to the character. He wore striped trousers from the off, but eventually changed from a lab coat into a jacket more akin to that of a 'redcoat' entertainer at a holiday camp – which he accessorized with a dapper black bowler hat. According to Joe's son Stephen, his dad also took some inspiration for Mr Tayto's image from the 'Striding Man', of Johnnie Walker whiskey fame.

The first mention of any name for this character came in 1957, when an ad referred to him as 'Sean Pud', aka 'S. Pud'. This was a once-off, with him more commonly referred to as 'The Tayto Man'. One 1959 ad for TaytoPak potatoes told consumers to 'Look for the Tayto Man on every bag' – but just a couple of months later, another ad for the same product told people to 'Look for the Mr Tayto trademark on every pack.' This was the first instance of this name and – from this point onward – it was a name that stuck. The character's public appeal was near instantaneous. In January 1958, Kerry man Mike McMahon won a prize for his 'Tayto-Man' costume at the annual fancy dress party in Killorglin. A few months later, elsewhere in Kerry, two children won a prize for their 'Tayto and Guinness' costume, beating off fierce competition from 'Mary and her Lamb' and 'Chinese Couple'.

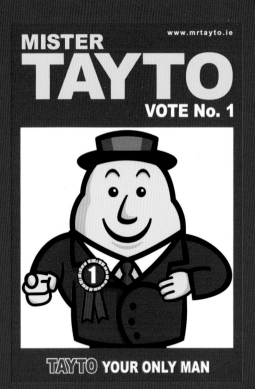

Mr Tayto's election posters (and manifestos) landed on poles across the nation in May 2007.

VOTE FOR TAYTO

It was only in the late noughties that Mr Tayto *really* came to life – all credit to the then-Taoiseach Bertie Ahern. In early 2007, Ray Coyle – who had just bought the company – and his team were brainstorming new marketing strategies to help remedy the fact that Tayto had been losing around 2 per cent of its market share per year. As they bandied about ideas towards the end of April, Ahern dissolved the Dáil, a general election was announced for the 24th of May, and Coyle had a brainwave, opting to take a page from Dustin the Turkey's playbook: Mr Tayto was going to run for election. A week later, Mr Tayto launched his campaign outside Leinster House, flanked by his election agent Frank Kelly (of *Father Ted* and Tayto gramophone fame) and armed with a battle bus, a series of posters, a website, and even a song – a trad-style singalong by The Roosters, entitled *Vote Mr Tayto No. 1*.

A refreshingly honest spokesperson for Tayto admitted, 'This stunt is purely a marketing gimmick to cash in on the general election fever and sell more crisps.' This ingenious guerilla marketing campaign saw Mr Tayto and Kelly canvassing the country, availing of free ad space on every lamp-post in the country, and becoming the focus of innumerable column inches – and then more again, after they received small fines for unauthorized postering. Along the way, Kelly – speaking on behalf of Mr Tayto, as he 'was afraid of being misquoted' – laid out his client's policies on topics like stamp duty ('there should be no obligation to buy stamps'), class sizes ('should never be under 12ft by 9ft'), greenhouse gases ('eliminate them by painting all houses red') and his cabinet ('solid mahogany with a lovely silver inlay'). Ultimately, Mr Tayto claimed several hundred – spoiled – votes around the country as Pat Stacey of the *Evening Herald* deemed him 'the only truly credible candidate in this election'. That June, 'Mr Tayto' was Ireland's most googled term and Tayto's receding market share was reversed.

'Mr Tayto, Mr Tayto, the snack that has the knack for havin' the craic. Vote for Tayto, Vote for Tayto, he'll always be the leader of the pack.'

MR TAYTO'S LONELY HEARTS CLUB

In January 2008, Mr Tayto embraced social media to hunt for a wife – or 'the cheese to his onion'. His 'Looking for Love' campaign was launched with a YouTube video showing the lonely fifty-something singleton dining alone in a restaurant, when he bears witness to a romantic marriage proposal. This heart-wrenching moment apparently motivated him to recruit actor Simon Delaney as his wingman, hire tailor Louis Copeland to cut him a fancy new version of his iconic suit, and place lonely hearts ads in the papers, directing potential suitors towards a website where they could apply to be Mrs Tayto. Together with Delaney, Ireland's most edible bachelor boarded the Love Bus for a nationwide tour of twenty towns and cities. Despite thousands of applicants, the campaign ended on the 19th of March with Mr Tayto issuing 'An Open Letter to the People of Ireland' – in which he admitted that he was 'not yet ready to settle down'. 'Variety is the spice of life', he wrote, 'and just like one day I might want Cheese & Onion and the next Salt & Vinegar, I don't think I can be just a one woman kind of guy.'

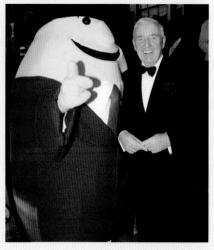

At the Bloom Festival 2014, Tayto Park landscaper David Everard won a silver-gilt medal for his Tayto garden, which used thousands of shrubs and plants to plot out the crisp-making process. The centrepiece of the installation was this seventeen- foot tall bush sculpture of Mr Tayto, which took pride of place in Tayto Park after the event. (Presence PR)

Mr Tayto with broadcasting legend Bill O'Herlihy. 'There's a big emotional connection to the character,' says Tayto managing director John O'Connor. 'You send him to a concert or to a football game, and grown people are racing over to get their photograph taken with him.' Some people, however, get *too* excited when they spot the potato gentleman. 'The worst thing was when a child tried to take a bite out of my arm,' according to somebody that once donned the costume. 'He had been threatening to do it earlier on in the day, so I should have listened to him.'

In 2010, Tayto announced their partnership with the Republic of Ireland men's national team, shortly before they qualified for the UEFA European Championship for the first time in twenty-four years. Lucky mascot Mr Tayto is pictured here alongside the squad, including manager Giovanni Trapattoni and star players including Robbie Keane, John O'Shea and Damien Duff. (Sportsfile)

Actor Frank Kelly and Mr
Tayto at the unveiling of
The Man Inside the Jacket
(Jason Clarke Photography)

MR TAYTO: LITERARY SENSATION

In October 2009, Mr Tayto capitalized on his growing fanbase and
his new life away from the packet by launching his own autobiography, *The Man Inside the Jacket*. According to Coyle's son, Charles,
'the idea of the book came about through the TV commercial that
he wanted to do for it'. Ray was an admirer of Hal Douglas – the
prolific voice actor who narrated thousands of movie trailers, from
Men in Black to *Marley & Me* – and 'wanted to use him in something'.
And so, he reverse-engineered the idea of a book, hiring Maïa
Dunphy to ghostwrite the mascot's satirical life story, along with
Ciaran Morrison (the legendary puppeteer and comic behind Zig
and Rodge) and Mick O'Hara (Zag and Podge). 'It is a story so
powerful,' begins Douglas's eventual voiceover for the book's
dramatic trailer, 'men have died to protect it.' Shane Hegarty of *The
Irish Times* deemed the spoof memoir to be 'only marginally less
legitimate than the autobiographies of various pop stars, models
and footballers', calling Mr Tayto 'a Forrest Gump-like figure,
popping up alongside major figures of the past few decades'.

That Christmas, shop bookshelves were filled with tomes about the banking crisis and the demise of the Celtic Tiger, and so Mr Tayto provided a welcome respite from all of the doom and gloom, referring to himself – through his literary agent Frank Kelly – as 'the book world's answer to Rage Against the Machine'. The book was available in over 1,000 outlets (including shops and service stations that didn't usually sell books) and featured on the side of twenty Tayto trucks. Around €800,000 was also spent on marketing, encompassing a publicity tour, billboards and cinema/ TV commercials. The book quickly became a bestseller, ultimately selling over 50,000 copies and spending six weeks at the top of the Non-Fiction charts, claiming the coveted Christmas number one spot in the process. 'That's right,' reiterates Mick O'Hara. 'A biography about a completely made-up, suit-wearing potato man was the number one "Non-Fiction" book in Ireland.' One of Maïa Dunphy's proudest moments came years later, when an alleged fact from the book turned up as an answer in a UK radio quiz. According to Dunphy's version of events, the first-ever six-pack of crisps was created on the day of Éamon de Valera's inauguration in 1959, when Mr Tayto's dad made crisps for the event and the new president asked for a few bags to take home. 'Obviously not true at all', says Dunphy, 'but a classic example of fake news!'

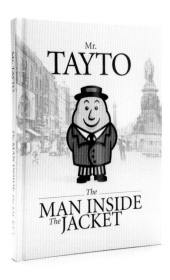

'Also, beating Bertie Ahern was another bit of joy!' says O'Hara. After accidentally kick-starting Mr Tayto's political career two years earlier, Ahern had since been forced to resign, before writing his autobiography – a much anticipated tell-all memoir that had been as good as guaranteed the top spot for Christmas. It wasn't to be, and the following year Mr Tayto would even cut the ribbon on his own theme park. The adorable spud's transformation from a hand-drawn emblem to a seal of quality and brand ambassador to a much-loved national jester, inside joke, father figure *and* rollercoaster tycoon was complete.

Throughout Tayto's first few decades, Joe Murphy was the affable, often eccentric public face of the company. Although intervening CEOs carried out their duties in a far quieter fashion, the 'Spud Murphy' role was one that Ray Coyle embraced during his own tenure. By pushing Mr Tayto to the forefront of the brand, Coyle had in essence installed him as the de facto head of the company, ensuring that Tayto will always have an omni-present figurehead to guide it into the future, come what may.

WHERE'S MR TAYTO?

In 2022, Mr Tayto vanished from his usual spot on the front of every Tayto packet. The Irish public was tasked with helping to find the AWOL mascot, by reporting any sightings of him to his keepers at Tayto. When he eventually resurfaced, it transpired that after two years cooped up during intermittent Covid lockdowns, he had gone off on a globetrotting, sightseeing adventure – travelling from Salthill to California, via NYC and Zimbabwe, crossing off places from his bucket list and racking up millions of TikTok views along the way.

(Verve Live Agency & Lost Studios)

TAYTO ON THE
SMALL SCREEN

A notice posted in several newspapers, to celebrate the fact that one of Tayto's very first TV ads won an award at the Cork Film Festival.

THE EARLY YEARS OF IRISH TV

On New Year's Eve 1961, Telefís Éireann started broadcasting to anybody lucky enough to be able to afford a TV. It opened with an address from President Éamon de Valera, and soon after came the first-ever advertisement to be beamed into living rooms across the country ... for cigarettes.

The much more family-friendly crisp ads weren't far behind though, and ever since then Tayto have been responsible for a number of era-defining ads, some of which have caused quite a stir around the water cooler. Within a couple of years of the launch of RTÉ, September 1963 would see Tayto picking up an award at the Cork Film Festival for their seven-second animation *Tayto Crisps Eater*. Another cartoon, also sadly lost to the sands of time, shows a scientist travelling into outer space in a rocket ship. 'All that he said when he got back', according to the accompanying jingle, 'is "Tayto are terrific".'

Another lost ad, this time from 1975, depicted the discovery of potato crisps 2,000 years ago, around the time of mythical warrior Cú Chulainn – an anachronism that drew the ire of one pernickety letter-writer into *The Irish Times*. Soon after came another animation, paired with a jingle that would worm its way in viewers' heads for decades to come. The ad introduced us to an anthropomorphic saltshaker and bottle of vinegar, both bearing a distinctly southern U.S. drawl. The ad saw them singing a duet, to the tune of the meandering nursery rhyme/scouts' chant 'Michael Finnegan' (he who had 'whiskers on his chin-egan').

If there had been any misconception that Tayto was a one-flavour wonder, this ditty firmly put that idea to bed, its infectious melody making mouths of a certain age salivate for Salt and Vinegar Tayto, to this very day.

I'm Old Dan Salt,
I'm Victor Vinegar,
The best darn taste
since time begin-egar,
Our crisps are the
outright win-egar,
Tayto Salt and Vinegar.

TAYTO'S SECRET MISSION

July 1985 saw the release of the fourteenth James Bond film, *A View to a Kill*. It was Roger Moore's final outing as 007, but it also saw Dublin actor Alison Doody making her silver screen debut, as 'Bond girl' Jenny Flex. Also that year, in what was unlikely to have been a coincidence, Doody starred in a stylish Tayto ad involving a secret agent on a secret mission. Late at night in some unnamed tropical location, Doody dramatically sneaks into a mystery office – presumably belonging to some sort of evil villain – and flips a hidden switch to reveal a safe. Within the safe is a scroll, a 'TOP SECRET' folder, and a bag of Tayto Cheese & Onion. Alas, an older moustachioed gentleman in a white tuxedo notices that there's an intruder in his office and catches Doody with his bag of Tayto. She hands him the packet, pops a crisp into his mouth, and vanishes into the night. He's so delighted to have rescued his precious crisps that he doesn't seem to notice – or care – that Doody has made off with his files. After all, confidential files are ten a penny, but a bag of Tayto in a foreign country is worth its weight in gold. 'So fresh they're irresistible,' says the narrator. 'Well, it's only what you'd expect from Tayto.' Alison Doody went on to star in *Indiana Jones and the Last Crusade*, *Taffin* and the Oscar-winning *RRR* – but it all started, as they say, with a crisp.

ATTACK A PACK

In 1989, Tayto launched their new look packet with 'Attack a Pack', which follows one teenager's continuous attempts to escape his group of friends, to avoid having to share any of his Tayto. His four unfortunate pals are clearly so accustomed to this behaviour that they've learned to stalk him with military-like precision and have even evolved the ability to stretch and flex their arms – akin to Mr Tickle – to ultimately gain access to the forbidden crisp packet from a distance. This game of cat-and-mouse is set to the beat of a very 80s hip-hop tune, featuring a strange pitched-down vocal effect.

I'm on my own, trying to find
A place where I can munch.
The reason is this pack you see,
And that hungry Tayto bunch.
Now I'm back here, out of sight,
With my favourite pack.
But I get a feeling, from behind,
Someone's planning a pack attack.
A Tayto attack,
A Tayto attack,
A Tayto attack ...
Attack a pack.

DERMOT CARMODY

In 1992, young comedian Dermot Carmody starred in a series of 'irreverent and sometimes nonsensical' skits in which he plays a Tayto-loving performer not lacking in self-confidence. According to copywriter Nick McGivney, these ads were his attempt 'to tie Tayto in to the then-nascent Irish alt-comedy scene.' In 'Blues', Carmody strums an acoustic guitar whilst dramatically telling the viewer that 'there are two things in my life more important to me than anything else: the blues, and Tayto.' Another spot, 'Poem', promises 'a short poem by Dermot Carmody.' Having swapped his business attire for a Victorian-style cravat, he recites his ode whilst holding a bag of Tayto like a proud father.

Because I could not stop for Death – He kindly stopped for me – The Carriage held but just Ourselves – And Immortality Tayto.

If that sounds in any way familiar, it *might* be because it's one of the most well-known verses in all of American literature. Not that our poet cares, smugly accepting a thin smattering of applause from his gullible audience – as Emily Dickinson scholars scream at the telly. Carmody's light-fingered approach to performance art continues into another sketch, a play on the classic 'Happiness is a cigar called Hamlet' commercials. As he attempts to regale the viewer with some bizarre-sounding anecdote, he runs into some technical difficulties with his microphone. He eventually gives up, produces a bag of Tayto from his inside pocket and enjoys an on-air snack to the gorgeous strains of Bach's 'Air on the G String' (as heard on the cigar ads). The TV advertising of tobacco had recently been outlawed, so this crisp-based parody cleverly adopted a piece of music that had been a television staple for the previous twenty-five years. 'We were really aiming to talk to kids,' says McGivney, 'as they hadn't been talked to by any of the big, familiar brands of the day.'

THE DEVIL'S TAYTO

On the 14th of May 1999, during the ad break of Gay Byrne's penultimate *Late Late Show*, Tayto launched one of the most daring, memorable and downright *terrifying* commercials of the 90s. The 'Hell' ad, which posed the question 'What would you do for the Tayto taste?', starred Lucifer himself – bearing more than a passing resemblance to Darkness, Tim Curry's nightmarish creature in the 1985 fantasy film *Legend*. Beneath the latex was Stephen Brennan, who had most recently been seen

on Irish screens as the technology obsessed Fr Niall Haverty in *Father Ted*. He was also a well-established theatre actor who had tread the boards of the Abbey and Gate theatres on numerous occasions – exactly the calibre of actor required to not only *portray* the Tayto-loving ruler of the bottomless pit, but to actually make the viewer *sympathize* with him.

We join him on a typical day at work, shattering the common workaday image of the Devil and showing his job to actually be quite mundane, largely consisting of paperwork and admin.

As he sorts through a never-ending queue of new arrivals, he fast tracks all of the usual suspects (thieves, lawyers, politicians, etc.) before being stopped in his tracks when faced with two seemingly pious nuns, halos and all. Unable to find their names in his big fiery book, he presumes that there's been an error and directs them towards the elevator to Heaven. Exhausted from all of this excitement, he pauses for a break and pulls out his lunchbox, which contains a sandwich, an apple and a Thermos. But missing from it is the most important element of any lunchbox. Having realized that he's been swindled, the Prince of Darkness howls in fury/hunger as the two nuns cackle maniacally in the lift towards the pearly gates, scoffing away on the stolen bag of Tayto.

In a follow-up spot, ol' Redface phones the angel Gabriel (whose hold music is the 'Hallelujah' chorus of Handel's *Messiah*), who promptly hangs up on him.

Stephen Brennan initally declined the offer to star in this spot, for fear that such a high profile ad could have a negative impact on his other acting opportunities. The ad's writer and creative director, Pearse McCaughey, managed to twist his arm, promising him that he'd be under such heavy prosthetics that 'nobody's gonna know who you are.' The morning after the commercial first aired, Brennan popped into a newsagent to pick up a packet of cigarettes. 'I saw you on the telly last night!' immediately chirped the woman behind the counter.

Behind the scenes on the set of 'Hell': actor Stephen Brennan takes a break from having his make-up applied by special FX wizards Mike Measimer and Tom McInerney.

'We only had the money to do one hand,' says creative director Pearse McCaughey, talking about the Devil's prosthetic fingers, 'so Stephen had to hide the other hand. Even though he's got the mask on, he actually communicates a range of emotions, and vocally he's brilliant.' (Tom McInerney)

TAYTO MATADOR

Another case study into the extremes that people would go to for the Tayto taste was the 2001 'Bull Fighter' ad, which involved the construction of a Spanish villa in Dublin. We meet a highly charged Spanish father – played by famed character actor John Kavanagh, as seen in epic historical sagas like *Braveheart* and *Alexander* – who tells us about his son José, aka 'the greatest bull-fighter in all of España'.

Because of this, Dad has been left baffled by José's decision to sacrifice all of his fame and glory to move to Ireland, of all places. We get a glimpse of the once-magnificent matador in his new environment, waving a red rag at a bemused cow at an auction in a Naas cattle mart. Why would any sane person embrace such an unglamorous career shift? All is revealed when we see him on his break, kissing and eating Tayto while professing his love for the crisps, in Spanish. Obviously the plain crisps of Spain were not sustenance enough for a top-flight matador like José.

This commercial somehow proved to be more controversial than 'Hell', with the Council Against Blood Sports calling the ad 'irresponsible' and claiming that it glamourized barbarism – despite the fact it doesn't actually feature any element of the questionable 'contest'. Tayto responded with a statement to clarify that it 'in no way supports or condones bull-fighting', which is not something that a crisp manufacturer has to do every day. Perhaps it could even be posited that José himself had come to his senses, and Ireland's plentiful Tayto supply was just *one* of the reasons why he needed to leave his former life behind.

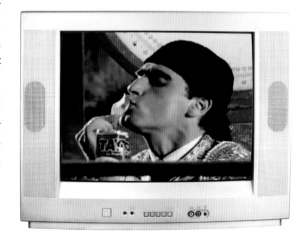

'From Sevilla to Barcelona, he is loved by millions. He has everything an hombre could wish for – women, money, fame, family who loves him.'

'Did you know that potatoes were first grown by ancient Incas in South America, and weren't discovered by Europeans until about 1554? Which is amazing, because exactly 400 years later they were perfected in Ireland with the invention of the original Cheese & Onion crisp. Just something to think about, next time you get caught eating a packet of Tayto in the back of history class.'

PERU, 1554

In 2002, we travelled to 16th-century Peru for an ad that told us 'There's no crisp like a Tayto crisp.' A cool modern-day youngster – complete with skateboard and earphones, schoolbag slung over one shoulder, time machine presumably just out of shot – walks and skates around Tawantinsuyu, giving us a history lesson. As he presents his spiel (see opposite), Spanish conquistadors arrive to pillage and plunder the serene little community in which he has found himself.

If you've been paying attention, you'll have noticed that the year of the discovery of the potato has been massaged by a couple of decades to allow for congruity with the invention of Tayto. You may *also* have observed the humble fact that this is Tayto's first-ever TV ad to mention their invention of Cheese & Onion – almost five decades later! The ad's end screen features a couple of golden Inca idols alongside five *Irish* ones – the three classic Tayto flavours, along with two brand new ones: Flame-Thrower Chilli and Kickin' Curry.

SHINE

This 2003 ad was a rare earnest addition to the Tayto canon. Soundtracked by a chilled-out acoustic rendition of 'This Little Light of Mine' (the tonal opposite of 'Attack a Pack'), we follow a hip young fellow around Dublin, armed with a bag of Tayto. As the narrator espouses the relatively low-salt, low-fat nature of Tayto cooked in pure sunflower oil, sunflowers begin to sprout from the ground beneath our hero. By the time he reaches O'Connell Bridge, he's passed so many other Tayto munchers, the city is overrun with van Gogh's favourite flower. Traffic has been brought to a standstill and Dublin resembles the Tuscan countryside more than any dirty old town. 'Small wonder three out of four people prefer them,' professes the narrator.

THERE'S ALWAYS ONE

In 2005, the 'Biggest Fan' ad took the form of a Gaelic football match, commentated on by GAA's most famous voice, the much-missed Mícheál Ó Muircheartaigh. The Irishness of it all was in stark contrast to the soccer-centric campaigns of Tayto's main rival at the time, whose fans this ad was a bit of a dig towards. As we join the match, the opening point has just been scored, which is not usually a moment of any significant excitement. However, one of the players on the Tayto-sponsored winning team obviously hasn't received the memo, and reacts as if they've just scored the winning goal in the last minute of the All-Ireland final. 'What's happening here now?' wonders Ó Muircheartaigh, watching the player pull his jersey over his head and emitting a gleeful battle cry. 'Well, three out of four people may prefer Tayto,' the commentator philosophizes, 'but there's always one.' Not only was this ad responsible for reintroducing a classic saying into the modern lexicon, but it managed to replace the original three-word phrase with 'As they say in the Tayto ad, "there's always one".' A follow-up ad, narrated by radio presenter Ian Dempsey, drove home this point, presenting us with another strange personality type. 'Hello' features four women enjoying a Tayto picnic in the park, playing a game of 'He loves me, he loves me not' with a sunflower (what else?). Alas, one of them spoils the mood by taking things too far:

'He loves me not ... yet. But he will when he sees me. I know where he lives, I know where he works, and one day I'm gonna go up to him and I'm just gonna say ... "helloooo".'

Although her friends laugh along, it was likely the last time they invited *her* on a picnic.

MR. TAYTO BROUGHT TO LIFE

As soon as the company is bought by Ray Coyle's Largo Foods, Mr Tayto's real-world, three-dimensional avatar takes on a life of its own. After his hugely successful election race/wife hunt/ memoir, the spud man found himself pushed into the forefront of anything and everything Tayto related. During this glorious new era, the focus of all Tayto advertising shifted towards building a mythology around the character and developing the relationship between him and all of his loyal denizens across the island.

MORE THAN JUST A CRISP

In 2015, Lorcan Finnegan – who would go on to direct acclaimed thriller films *Vivarium, Nocebo* and *The Surfer* – made the 'More Than Just a Crisp' ads, in which Mr Tayto is presented not merely as a crisp salesman but as an omniscient guardian angel. This ad depicts his tendency to show up out of the blue to save the day and/or prevent people from making terrible, regrettable decisions. Take, for example:

A dishevelled woman – all messy hair and leisurewear – is nipping home from the shop when she spots her dream fella. What if he sees her in this state?! Luckily, Mr Tayto pulls her behind a bush and out of view, just before the hunk looks around.

An insecure young fellow disrobes in a solarium, before Mr Tayto arrives to teach him a lesson: it's not a sun bed he needs, it's a bag of Tayto. Mr Tayto reassuringly pats the lad's knee as he munches and weeps away.

A titillated young man is about to post a questionable comment ('I wish I was that blanket') under somebody's beach pic. Right in the nick of time, a disapproving Mr Tayto magics himself into his bedroom and yanks the computer's plug out of its socket.

THE TRUE TASTE OF HOME

'The True Taste of Home' (2023) was a documentary-style clip beginning with a middle-aged couple at the airport, eagerly awaiting the arrival of their long-absent daughter, Aoife. Dad has even brought along a Tupperware box full of biscuits that he spent all night baking. They can't contain their delirium when their child finally enters the arrivals hall ... and neither can she. However, it's not *them* that she's most excited to be reunited with. Aoife runs straight past her father's open arms – knocking into him, sending his tub of bickies flying – and straight into the warm embrace of that seven-foot tall yellow spud that we all know and love (some more than others, it seems). She and her beau happily squeeze into the backseat of Dad's car, while her folks look mortified about the unannounced plus-one – especially given the presence of the camera crew. They look so peeved that they probably wish she'd just stayed wherever she was. There's nothing like Tayto to bring a family together, eh!

Mr Tayto didn't *only* greet 'Aoife' at the airport. As part of the 'True Taste of Home' campaign, he welcomed home thousands of people – at the arrival gates at Dublin Airport – with hugs, high fives and free packets of Tayto. (Publicis)

Mission Accomplished: Mr Tayto heading home from the North Pole, after having made sure that Santa wouldn't be left empty-handed on Christmas morning.

EVERYONE GETS A GIFT

Later in 2023, Tayto finally gave the nation something that it had been waiting sixty-nine festive seasons for: a heart-warming Christmas ad. In 'Everyone Gets a Gift', we join an exhausted Santa Claus as he arrives home to Lapland after another action-packed Christmas Eve spent hopping up and down a few billion chimneys. As usual, he's the only person in the world without a present under *his* tree. Despite being a selfless old soul who's been doing this job since time immemorial, he still looks somewhat disappointed that *he* doesn't have a Santa. However, as he snoozes … in his armchair by the fire, a mystery figure pays him a visit. When Old Saint Nick awakens, he discovers that he's not the *only* big jolly man in red who likes to spread happiness and good cheer. It turns out that none other than Mr Tayto himself has swung by the North Pole to deliver the most Irish of Christmas gifts – a festive box of Cheese & Onion crisps. 'It wouldn't be Christmas without Tayto,' proclaims the end screen of an ad which seems certain to become a Christmas tradition in itself.

MOVING TO
MEATH

(Simon McDermott, Leinster Photographic)

THE HEIR TO THE CRISP THRONE

Ray Coyle, the owner of Largo Foods and now Tayto, had history with Tayto – as well as more than a few entrepreneurial characteristics reminiscent of one Joe Murphy. 'He reminded me an awful lot of my father,' says Joe's son Stephen. 'He was the same type of man, cut from the same cloth.'

Coyle grew up on a tillage and cattle farm in Curragha, just a fifteen-minute walk from where Tayto HQ now stands. His family also owned the local pub, Paud O'Donoghue's Forge, where he was born in 1951. At the age of twenty-one, he started growing his own potatoes on six acres of family land, selling them to a Dublin merchant at £6 per tonne. By 1976, drought on mainland Europe had helped to inflate the price of spuds to £150 per tonne and Coyle had a turnover of around £1 million per year – as well as around 800 acres of his own farmland, and a contract supplying potatoes to Tayto. However, if the world of potatoes is known for anything, it's for being unpredictable. The price of spuds collapsed in the late 70s, Coyle lost his Tayto contract a couple of years later, and he found himself owing the banks well over a million quid.

Spurning the idea of a traditional land sale, Coyle's flair for left-brain thinking became apparent when he opted instead to organize a raffle, to be hosted by broadcaster Mike Murphy at Goffs auction house. For £300, punters were in with a chance of winning 365 acres of land at Bellewstown Estate in Meath. Coyle sold around 2,600 tickets, taking in far more than the £350,000 that the land was worth. After paying off his debts, he decided that instead of supplying potatoes to crisp companies, he'd supply them to ... himself. In 1983, he founded Largo Foods and started making 'Cottage Crisps' – but business got off to a slow start, largely due to the dominance of Tayto. 'Like everything else,' he later reflected, 'you jump in and you find that there isn't as much money in it as you thought and that it's harder than it looked and it takes a long time to build up the business. It wasn't until I bought the Perri brand that things took off.' Although Perri had been off the market for over a decade, Coyle resuscitated the name to some success. Years later, in 1996, Coyle would also buy Sam Spudz in Gweedore, Donegal – then on the brink of collapse – as well as launching his own 'Hunky Dorys' crisps.

In 2006, having just bought Tayto, Coyle realized that leaning into the Irish wit and storytelling tradition was key to competing with the big budget multinationals – Proctor & Gamble, PepsiCo and United Biscuits – that owned their main competitors. Tayto was reborn with a series of light-hearted, anarchic marketing campaigns, painstakingly planned but delivered in an appealingly freewheeling fashion – as well as its very own theme park. All of this exposure racked up a huge amount of unpaid publicity, through public conversation and media commentary. From 2008 to 2010, Tayto jumped from tenth to fifth place in *Checkout Magazine*'s Top 100 Brands list. By 2021, Tayto would be in second place, just behind Coca-Cola.

Unfortunately for Coyle, his purchase of Tayto closely coincided with the global financial crisis, which was well underway by 2007 – a year that also saw the price of raw materials increase significantly. Saddled with debt and in need of capital to complete what would become Tayto Park, he sought and engaged a partner in the Intersnack Group. He initially sold 15 per cent of the company, before becoming a minority shareholder in 2011 and selling his remaining stake in 2017.

In 2019, Largo Foods – by now encompassing the Irish pursuits of Tayto, King, Hunky Dorys, Perri, O'Donnell's, Pom-Bear, Hula Hoops and KP – rebranded as 'Tayto Snacks', in an 'homage to the strength, longevity and recognition' of Joe Murphy's brand. Despite challenges posed by Brexit and Covid-19, Tayto would see continued growth and an increase in sales into the 2020s.

'I came across Hersheypark in Pennsylvania, built by Milton Hershey, the owner of the Hershey chocolate factory. He built it as a place for his employees and their families to relax. Over time, it grew to become a major tourist attraction. And Anheuser-Busch did Busch Gardens. I decided I wanted to build a similar type theme park, based around the Tayto brand.'

TAYTO PARK

When it came to introducing something distinctly American to Irish shores for the first time, opening up a snack-themed amusement park was not Ray Coyle's first rodeo. The story of Ireland's first-ever theme park begins in 1996, with a once-endangered, horned beast – when Coyle decided to transplant twenty-eight bison from the dry plains of North America (via Belgium) to the soggy fields of south-east Meath. This purchase would go on to have a monumental impact on Ireland's tourism and snack industries. Over the years, an increasing number of curious folk took to trespassing on to the Coyles' land, peeping over the hedges in the hope of catching a glimpse of the fabled herd of bison. Noticing this one day, Ray's son Charles casually suggested that they should open up some sort of a visitors' park. Ray, inspired by the dusty Americana evoked by the bison, envisioned a pleasure ground with a 'Wild West' theme.

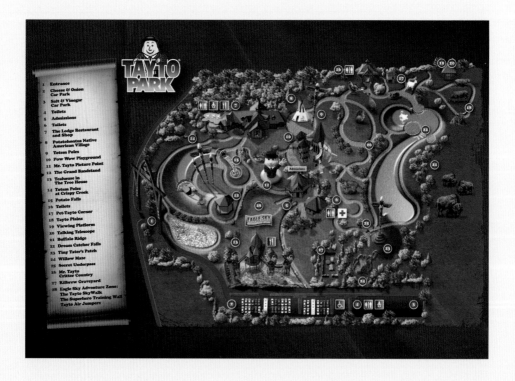

By 2007, after Coyle had spent years buying up as many fields adjacent to his factory as possible, his now 300-strong bison herd had a 141-acre parcel of land to call home. By this point, Ray had *another* major asset in his back pocket: ownership of a brand that – more than just a household name – was a cultural institution. He took out his chequebook, signed away almost ten million euro, and set about landscaping fifty-five acres of farmland into the ultimate family day trip destination. As he looked into importing totem poles from Vancouver, he also registered a business name for his new enterprise: the humbly titled 'Ashbourne Visitor Centre Ltd'.

Behold a decade of huge progress: On the left the Tayto Park map from when it first opened in 2010. On the right the 2022 map (just before it changed its name to Emerald Park).

On a cold, *crisp* Wednesday on the 24th of November 2010, Tayto Park opened its gates for the first time. Three days later, Santa Claus himself arrived to visit the amazing new park. However, along with Santy came a Big Freeze that would go down in history, as thick blankets of snow covered the country and Met Éireann reported some of our lowest-ever temperatures – not exactly ideal conditions for a weather-dependent outdoor attraction. *Also* within a month of opening day, the Irish government agreed to a three-year bailout programme with the European Central Bank, and declared that harsh austerity measures would need to be imposed on the public. Coyle feared the worst: that he'd lose his biggest ever gamble, and that his many naysayers would be proven right.

> 'Everybody thinks you're bonkers until you make a thing work.'

Fast forward a few months, to April 2011, and everything changed, all at once. Over the Easter holidays, an unprecedented 25,000 people showed up, with kids racing each other from the Cheese & Onion Car Park (or the Salt & Vinegar Car Park, depending on your preference) into Mr. Tayto's glorious new kingdom. A TV ad had seen Mr Tayto gallivanting around the park in a safari suit, along with a warning – 'Not For Couch Potatoes' – to let people know what they were in for. After getting lost in the Willow Maze and wearing yourself out on the slides and climbing walls of the Pow Wow Playground, you could hop on over to Pet-Tayto Corner and Critter Country to admire pot-bellied pigs, pygmy goats, ocelots, pheasants, hens, geese, rabbits and rare birds – or observe the famous bison of Buffalo Ridge through a talking telescope. If crisps weren't nourishment enough, you could have a sit-down meal in either The Lodge restaurant or in the Teahouse in the Tree House (built into an old sycamore tree). Within the six tipis of Potatohontus Native American Village, you could get your face painted, adopt a balloon animal, listen to a storyteller, or catch a magic show. There were even a couple of picturesque man-made lakes, where you could admire Crispy Creek, Potato Falls and Dream Catcher Falls. The latter falls even offered you the chance to make a wish, which was nearly guaranteed to come true – assuming, of course, that your wish was to take a selfie with Mr Tayto.

In 2013, the then Taoiseach Enda Kenny visited the Tayto factory as seventy-eight new jobs were announced between the factory and Tayto Park. Pictured is Raymond Coyle taking him on the grand tour. 'I'm delighted that Tayto, as an Irish food icon, continues to grow strongly,' said Kenny. 'I'm a cheese and onion man,' he later remarked. (Photocall)

Visitors wanting to lean into the park's theme a little bit further could venture across a narrow country road, and into the place where the magic happens. The factory tour used interactive audio-visual displays to teach guests about the history of Tayto and the crisp-making process, with projections to make themselves feel like a crisp upon a conveyor belt. Windows overlooking the factory floor helped to give an elevated view of the workers and machinery in action. This self-guided tour was soundtracked by a reworked rendition of Ottawan's cheesy – and oniony – 1979 mega hit 'D.I.S.C.O.'.

Exiting the park at the end of a long, exciting day, you were sent on your merry way with a free six-pack of Tayto. In the midst of one of the worst-ever recessions, Tayto Park offered cash-strapped Irish families a fun-filled day out on a budget – which is why 224,000 people came to visit by the end of 2011. By the end of the decade, that annual total would have tripled. For Coyle, it was his first-ever business venture to be profitable within its first year, hushing the doubters and emboldening him to invest in it further. In the early days, the park was more akin to other super-playgrounds geared towards a younger audience, like Fort Lucan or Clara Lara. Ray, however, always had an eye towards the type of amusement park that only existed further afield.

And so, it was only in 2014 – when construction began on the country's first ever rollercoaster – that the grown-ups of Ireland sat up straight and realized that they could potentially have their very own *proper* theme park on their hands. Whereas Ray's original inspiration – Hersheypark – had received delivery of its first rollercoaster in 1923, seventeen years after opening, it had only taken Tayto Park five. In keeping with the natural, rustic look of the park, The Cú Chulainn Coaster was constructed out of yellow pine and became the biggest wooden rollercoaster with an inversion in Europe, upon its opening in June 2015. The ride, sitting on the banks of the River Hurley, took its name from one of Ireland's greatest folk heroes – a brave warrior whose weapon of choice was, incidentally, a hurley. By now, further expansion had seen the introduction of more animals (including birds of

It is 'T'... tasty.
It is 'A'... amazing.
It is 'Y'... yummy yummy.
It is 'T'... tantalizing.
It is oh-oh-oh...
T.A.Y.T.O.
T.A.Y.T.O.

prey, leopards and macaques), a circus, a steam train, a driving school for children, a zip-line, a 5-D cinema, junior thrill rides, and other white-knuckle rides like The Rotator and Endeavour. In 2017, Viking Voyage was unveiled – an extreme water ride in which visitors travel upon a Viking ship on an epic and treacherous journey around the coast of ancient Ireland. Along the way, you are brought back in time by the native woodland, wattle fencing, thatched huts, an eighteen-metre high mountain, and one of the first round towers to be built on the island in 900 years.

Interestingly, this round tower wasn't Tayto Park's only connection to the past. Within the grounds of the park is Kilbrew Graveyard, where many of the gravestones date back centuries. And in the north-west of the grounds are two ring ditches constructed during the Middle Bronze Age, at least 3,000 years ago. From this site, archaeologists have unearthed a ceramic urn filled with ashes, a bronze razor, a bone pin and animal bones likely to have been leftovers from a funerary feast. On the other side of the River Hurley, just outside the park perimeter, are two ancient henge monuments. It's clear that history has been getting made in this area for many millennia – so you can only wonder what the people in the urn would think if they could see the place now, their old fields filled with gravity-defying rides and the mouth-watering smell of crisps in the air.

With around 40 per cent of the park's guests visiting from outside of the Republic of Ireland, it had even been hailed in parliament as one of the main incentives of cross-border travel; in a 2018 Oireachtas speech, Senator Frank Feighan noted that 'the two Ts' (Tayto Park and Titanic Belfast) 'have certainly brought the people of the island together.' So when, in 2022, it was announced that Tayto Park would be changing its name, crisp-loving thrill-seekers all over the island were heart-broken. It was, however, a tough but necessary decision so that the park and Tayto Snacks could each pursue new opportunities, after a fruitful twelve-year partnership.

The shortlist of potential new names included Lands of Adventure, Megaland, Legends Park, Park of Legends, Top Park, Curragha Park and Mí Park – but on New Year's Day 2023, Mr. Tayto's former empire was rebranded as 'Emerald Park'. Just like Landsdowne Road and The Point Depot (which were both demolished in 2007), there'll always be some stubborn folk who insist on calling it by its original name. It wouldn't be Ireland otherwise! Thankfully this break-up was an amicable one, and a full range of Tayto snacks is still available for purchase in the Emerald Park gift shop – still freshly produced daily, in the factory next door.

As thrill seekers ascend The Cú Chulainn Coaster, they pass each of the thirty-two county flags of Ireland – before letting gravity bring them back to earth at a speed of ninety kilometres per hour. (Photocall)

WHAT GOES INTO MAKING THE NATION'S FAVOURITE CRISPS?

THE PROCESS

THE KEY INGREDIENT

Every stage of the crisp-making process, from seed potato to shop shelf, has an impact on the type of crisp that reaches the consumer. Tayto provide their growers with seeds and expert advice on all aspects of potato production, from the ploughing stage to harvesting and storage. This advice covers everything from weed control methods to the width of the drills and the space between the tubers. However, the most crucial, and unpredictable, element is the weather – specifically the Irish weather. Seed potatoes are planted between St Patrick's Day and May, and then harvested over September and October – meaning that potato supply is at its lowest in the summertime, when Tayto demand is often at its highest. Growing the perfect Tayto potatoes calls for a Goldilocks-style perfect balance of conditions. Dry summers result in a low yield of small potatoes, whereas wet summers result in a large yield – but also digging difficulties, the potential for blight, and excess dirt making it into the factory. Cold summers can also provide a curveball, as temperatures of less than 7°C can cause a build-up of sugar in the potatoes, resulting in blackened crisps. Potatoes also need to be buried deep and then stored in a dark place, as light exposure produces chlorophyll, which can lead to the dreaded green crisp.

The main varieties of potato that Tayto use today are Beo, Kiebitz, Edony and the three Ladies (Lady Claire, Lady Jo and Lady Rosetta). These are all round, light-coloured potatoes ideal for crisping and grown by a number of farmers across Meath, Dublin, Louth and Wexford. One of the longest-serving and biggest suppliers is Ivan Curran of Broadleas Farm in Stamullen, not far from Tayto HQ. Ivan's father Jimmy secured a contract with Tayto in the 1970s, and now one third of the 2,000 acre family farm is dedicated to the mighty spud. Ivan supplies Tayto with around 60 per cent of his total potato crop – 5,000 tonnes of potatoes – per year.

Another local farmer that followed the family trade is Anthony Battersby of Rice's Hill Farm, less than two kilometres from Tayto HQ. Having taken over from his father Tony, Anthony has been supplying Tayto for over three decades, dedicating around 450 acres of land to growing future crisps. (Sean Breithaupt)

Meath farmer Ivan Curran, one of Tayto's longest-serving and biggest suppliers.

Potatoes are brought to the factory as they're required, usually a couple of times per day. Before crossing the threshold, all potatoes are inspected for blight, rot, greening, size, sugar content and dry matter. They enter the factory on a vibrating belt, which removes the small potatoes, then enter a large washer that cleans the potatoes and removes any excess clay. The potatoes are then put through a polisher which gives them a final brush, before entering the main peelers. Once peeled, they are sliced and washed to remove any excess starch and fried in sunflower oil at 180c. Once the golden potatoes leave the fryer they are flavoured in rotating drums and packed into bags.

FIGURE 3.3   POTATO CRISPS PRODUCTION SCHEMATIC

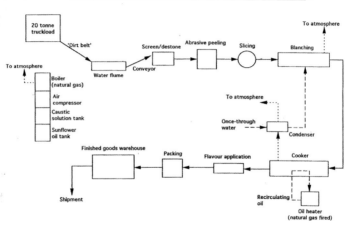

To produce 'extruded' snacks like Mighty Munch and Snax, powdered raw materials – usually maize grits or potato granules – are introduced to the extruder via a hopper (an inverted cone-shaped device), along with water and air. The dough is then formed into the shape of a bicycle wheel, a waffle, a burger, a monster's paw, a banshee's bone, or whatever you're having yourself. These pieces are then cyclone-blown to a hot air dryer, which reduces the moisture content from 12 per cent to 2 per cent before being fried or baked – causing them to expand into a crunchy puff. Flavouring is then applied in the same manner as it is for the crisps.

THE PACKAGING

For its first decade of operation, Tayto packaged its crisps in air-, water- and grease-resistant glassine paper bags. These were supplied by Bailey Gibson and Jefferson Smurfit, and sealed initially by hand, then by machine. The orange-tinged bag featured the Tayto logo in faintly tiger-patterned lettering. This packaging design changed very little during this time, aside from the addition of a small, inconspicuous Mr Tayto in the early 60s.

In 1964, Tayto purchased their first automatic packing machine and introduced a new packaging material. These new MXXT ('moisture-proof saran coated cellophane') packets kept crisps fresh for longer, increasing their shelf life. They were also partly transparent, with a little window through which the crisps were visible – a real novelty, especially for children, who were often fascinated by Tayto packets, which they interacted with in curious ways.

For some kids, it became a little game to hold the empty packet over an open fire and watch it melt and shrink down. They might then stick a pin to the back of the solidified plastic lump, et voilà ... free Tayto badge! 'We did that too,' confirms one child of the 70s. 'My mother used to go mad.' Others would take a magnifying glass and compete with their friends to see who could be the first to burn around the little drawing of Mr Tayto, freeing him from the packet. There was even a folk belief amongst some kids that the crisps tasted better if you opened the bag upside down. The Tayto packet designs of the 80s and 90s also featured an interesting optical illusion, and the most prominent Irish example of what is known as the 'Droste effect'. On the front of the packet, Mr Tayto was shown holding a bag of Tayto, which in turn featured a smaller image of himself holding a bag of Tayto... and so on, in a loop that potentially went on forever. Many children of this generation recall staring at their crisp packet, scratching their heads , contemplating infinity for the very first time.

STAYING FRESH

In 1996, Tayto swapped out their cellophane bags in favour of foil packaging. As well as being a heat-resistant material, foil is impermeable to light, air and moisture – which gave the crisps an even more extended shelf life. The shiny, reflective bags also had an eye-catching advantage, helping them to stand out in shop displays, where they would find themselves surrounded by hundreds of other brightly coloured competing products.

There was even a folk belief amongst some kids that the crisps tasted better if you opened the bag upside down.

In 2002, the packet was redesigned with a 'smile' insignia to accentuate the brand's friendly personality, and with more of a focus on Mr Tayto. According to one of the redesigners, Mr Tayto 'represents much of Tayto's Irish identity, and research pointed to a huge amount of equity in the little guy. But Mr Tayto had become tired and slightly lost in the existing packaging.' He was redrawn and placed in the centre of the pack, holding the Tayto logo, to ensure instant recognition of the Tayto brand and to create cohesion across the by-then vast product range. To coincide with Seachtain na Gaeilge 2013, Tayto launched a limited edition six-pack with retro 80s-style packaging and 'Cáis agus Oinniún' emblazoned on the front. In 2017, it was announced that all future Tayto packets would list the flavour in both Irish and English.

It's often said that you can guess somebody's age based on the lowest price of a bag of Tayto that they can remember. Joe Murphy 'was very conscious about pricing', according to his son, Barry. 'He always said to me, "It's easier to do a million one-dollar deals than one million-dollar deal."' Joe's approach to business explains why he occasionally felt the need to print notices in the newspapers, to remind customers and retailers about his company's preferred selling price. Like everything else, the price of a packet has changed over the years, as a result of inflation and various other market factors – including everything from potato shortages to oil strikes (like the one in Drogheda in 1965, that even forced chippers across the country to close their doors).

Within a few Decembers of its launch, Tayto was taking out newspaper ads suggesting that an eighteen-packet tin would be a mightily useful thing to have in the house for Christmas. The 'Crispmas Box' of Tayto quickly became an Irish festive tradition – as did leaving a packet by the fireplace for Ol' Saint Nick.

THE CLASSIC CRISPS

Upon its launch in 1954, Tayto was available in three flavours: Plain, Cheese, and Cheese & Onion. The Cheese flavour was discontinued within a couple of years, due to the public's disproportionate preference for Cheese & Onion. This preference also impacted sales of the Plain flavour, and eventually led to its decline. In fact, there are large chunks of the Irish population for whom Cheese & Onion crisps *are* 'Plain', such is the ubiquity of the default national flavour. In a 1970 letter to the *Irish Press*, a Mr John Vaughan complained that 'Crisps are offered today with salt-and-vinegar, cheese-and-onion flavour and various other flavours. Would it be too much to ask the manufacturers to provide a simple potato-flavoured crisp?' In the same newspaper, two days later, Joe Murphy himself responded to say 'Please tell Mr. John Vaughan not to lose heart. We have been manufacturing "Plain" unflavoured crisps for fifteen years now and shall continue to do so. Since our introduction of the "Cheese & Onion" flavoured crisp, nobody seems to love the "Plain" crisp anymore! Maybe it's the name. Can your readers think of a better one?' No suggestions were forthcoming, and the flavourless crisp was soon retired – much to the chagrin of journalist Kevin Myers, who wrote several articles in The Irish Times complaining about how Ireland was seemingly the only country in the world where you couldn't buy Plain crisps. Upon querying the issue with Tayto, he was told 'We have to have at least half a day's production to make it worthwhile commercially. But we wouldn't sell that much in four weeks, so we only do special orders for hotels and so on – and pack them in boxes, not bags.'

Three new flavours – Smokey Bacon, Crispy Sausage and Salt & Vinegar – were introduced to the range in the mid- to late-60s. The Crispy Sausage flavour was short-lived, and was replaced with the even *more* short-lived Celery flavour. In the ensuing decades, Tayto tended to stick to a small range of crowd-pleasing flavours, compared to some other, more experimental crisp companies. 'That's not to say we don't look for new flavours,' according to one-time sales and marketing director Kevin Masterson, a Tayto employee from 1960 right through into the 21st century. 'We're constantly monitoring and testing new flavours to see the reactions. We're constantly looking for other markets, monitoring what's going on. Over the years, we've gained experience about what the Irish consumer likes.'

Since the late 90s, the Tayto palate has extended to include a much broader range of crisps – beginning with Sour Cream and Onion (1997), Wor'ster Sauce (1999) and then two spicy flavours in 2002: Flame-Thrower Chilli and Kickin' Curry. Prawn Cocktail came along in 2006, with the late noughties also seeing the reintroduction of 'Plain' crisps, under the guise of a 'Ready Salted' flavour. This was again phased out, before being re-reintroduced in 2021, as 'Salted', alongside a relaunched Sour Cream and Onion flavour.

In the 2010s, the focus shifted towards 'limited edition' varieties that aimed to replicate popular dishes – from traditional Irish recipes (Irish Beef Stew, Bacon and Cabbage) to American sides and sandwiches (Hot Wings, Philly Cheese Steak, Beef Brisket, Bacon Melt), festive fare (Turkey and Stuffing) and even Chinese-style cooking (Spare Rib). In 2018, four new Irish-inspired flavours battled it out at a series of roadshows around the country. Tayto fans were invited to come along for a taste of four new flavours – Breakfast Roll, Spice Bag, Sunday Roast and Curry Sauce – before voting for their favourite. Spice Bag won with 51 per cent of the vote, and was therefore mass-produced and hit the shops. The following year, the second-place Curry Sauce flavour was refined into the 'Curry Chip' flavour and also launched nationwide.

In 2012, the Republic of Ireland football team qualified for the UEFA European Championship for the first time in over two decades. To mark the occasion, Tayto launched a 'Sour Cream and Dunne'ion' flavour, named in honour of star defender Richard Dunne. In tribute to forward Kevin Doyle, the packet claims that these crisps had been cooked in pure 'Sunflower Doyle'.

A real anomaly. This packet of Tayto (c. 2000) was made to be exported to a territory where a different company owns the Tayto name.

In 2022, Tayto set out to combine sweet and savoury by way of 'a crisp that tastes like a fizzy cola bottle': the controversial Fizzy Cola flavour. 'Our national vegetable has been defiled,' was the verdict of one taste tester for *The Irish Times*. Tayto Fizzy Cola was one of the fastest selling and most talked about Limited Editions the company ever had. In 2023, a slightly more obvious crossover led to Meanies flavoured crisps. The recontextualisation of the pungent pickled onion flavour on to a potato crisp – as opposed to a maize puff – resulted in a completely different snack, and received a much more favourable reaction from the public.

In what has become something of an annual tradition, 2024 saw Tayto self-collaborating again, creating a Mighty Munch flavoured crisp. According to Managing Director John O'Connor, these flavours are one of the ways in which Tayto connects and engages with the public. 'Creating excitement in the category,' according to O'Connor, 'presents an opportunity to engage new audiences, generate talkablity and demonstrate the brand's continued relevance.' A prime example of Tayto's special connection to the public is the case of Corkwoman Kaye Morrissey. In 2009, she texted into 2FM's Gerry Ryan Show, to lament the disappearance of Spring Onion Tayto – her flavour of choice throughout the 90s. Her text resulted in Tayto relaunching the crisps, with Morrissey enjoying an all-expenses paid trip to Dublin to be the first to try them.

In 2010, Tayto was launched in Shanghai under the name 'Tǔdòu Shēnshì Shǔpiàn', which roughly translates as 'Potato Gentleman Crisps'. Pictured here are the Salted and Thai Sweet Chilli flavours. Ever the ingenious business mind, Ray Coyle discovered that many shipping containers from China to Ireland are unloaded and then sent back to China empty – so the cost of sending a container-load of crisps to China actually worked out at around the same price as sending a container to London.

SNACKS AND FUN FOODS

Because so many now-standard chocolate bars were introduced in the 1930s, author and chocolate-lover Roald Dahl once claimed that 'the 30s is to chocolate' what 'the Italian Renaissance is to painting'. The same could be said of the 70s and iconic crunchy corn snacks. The huge new Coolock factory – along with the newly acquired factory in Inchicore – meant that for the first time in its history, Tayto had caught up with demand and was free to explore new products and ideas. It also had a burgeoning relationship with Beatrice Foods and Beatrice's family of pioneering food producers across the globe. Having already introduced Pete's Peanuts, salted popcorn ('Indian Popcorn') and sweet popcorn ('Totem Popcorn') in the 60s, the Tayto range *really* started to expand rapidly from the moment that they bought their first extruded snacks production line from Adams Corporation.

When journalist Gerry Byrne met Joe Murphy in his Coolock factory, Joe excitedly told him that they were in the process of building a £400,000 extension to house new equipment that would enable them to expand their 'Fun Foods' range – including something that he had tentatively called 'a wiggledy-waggledy', on account of its shape. It's unknown whether the wiggledy-waggledy ever made it to shop shelves, but plenty of others certainly did.

Joe would often call upon his kids and their friends to serve as focus groups for new snacks and flavours. They enthusiastically declared each prototype to be either 'Yuck', 'Nice' or 'Mmmmm' – the top grade implying that the crisp was so delicious that it had rendered their mouths incapable of saying actual words.

A Tayto stall from the late 60s, featuring all of the classics alongside the lesser-sighted Celery Tayto, Cheese Popples (a cheese puff snack) and Drink-Mix (sachets of powder to be mixed into water – available in Orange, Lemon, Raspberry, Strawberry and Cherry flavours). Multipack boxes of Tayto, known as a 'ParTpak', came with a free bag of popcorn.

The first extruded snack to be produced in Ireland was Snax in 1971 – a curved potato puff available in either Cheese & Onion or Smokey Bacon flavour. This was soon followed by the French-inspired Jonnie Onion Rings, and then Waffles (a bacon-flavoured potato snack, in the shape of a Belgian waffle), Spud-niks (a baked French fry, seasoned with salt and vinegar), Korn Kurls (a cheese puff), Bar-B-Que Kurls, Chickaroos (chicken flavoured corn pellets) and Zonkers (an all-dressed flavour corn snack, tasting almost like an early version of Monster Munch). In the 80s, the addition of the old Smith's factory in Terenure brought with it Chipsticks (salt and vinegar flavoured potato-and-corn sticks) and Monster Munch (a spicy replica of a monster's three-toed hoof). Not all of these snacks would last the test of time, mainly due to there being a limit on how many product lines Tayto could manufacture and market at once – as well as space constraints in the delivery vans and shop shelves. The ensuing years saw the launch of Wheelies (crispy bacon flavoured bicycle wheels), Snaps (pickled onion-flavoured crocodile jaws), Rondos (cheese and onion-flavoured potato rings), Toobs (salted potato rings) and Tayto Gators (another crocodile-themed snack, this time 'barbeque bacon' flavour). In the meantime, the King factory had started producing French Fries (similar to Chipsticks, available in Salt & Vinegar or Smokey Bacon) and King Kong (smokey bacon flavour) in 1976, before going on to make Chickatees (which replaced Chickaroos), Amigos (bacon and beans flavour), Saucy Devils and Doodaz – and later, another firm favourite called 'Crun-chos', an almost impossibly crunchy 'American-style' fried corn snack with a 'hot dog flavour'.

By the time that Raymond Coyle bought Tayto in 2006, he was already the owner of the Sam Spudz (Burger Bites) and Perri (Banshee Bones, Hot Lips, Thai Rings, Onion Rings) brands. And so, production of these snacks was moved to Tayto. Then, when Tayto became part of the Intersnack family (which also includes KP), it also took over production of Meanies, Mega Meanies, Rancheros and Skips. Mr Tayto duplicated and downsized himself in 2011 to create Mini Me's (tiny cheese and onion-flavoured Mr Taytos), and in 2021, production commenced on Cheesatees, a baked cheese snack with a 'big cheese flavour'. Tayto's penchant for limited-edition releases continued into 2024, when it launched spicy 'Tayto Hearts' just in time for Valentine's Day.

SOPHISTICATED SNACKS

Over the decades, Tayto also launched a number of products aimed more squarely at the adult consumer. They launched Special Chippies in the early 1960s, followed by extra strong Pub Crisps a couple of years later. Although these were the very same crisps, they came in a bigger, share-size packet without a printed price tag on the front. This was to give each individual publican freedom as to their pricing. The classic pairing of a pint and a packet of crisps shared amongst pals inspired the national pub tradition of carefully tearing open the bag of Tayto as if unfurling a picnic blanket – to reveal an Irish charcuterie board that barely lasts a few sips of stout.

Pictured in 1972, Olympic runner Ron Delany (centre) helps to launch a Pub Crisps competition, with the top prize being a trip to that summer's Munich Olympics. Having won gold at the 1956 Melbourne Olympics, Delany would remain the reigning Irish Olympic champion until Michael Carruth in 1992.

CHEESE & ONION

With managing director Vincent O'Sullivan pointing out that 'the adult sector within crisps and snacks is a growing European trend', the 1980s saw fancy dinner party crisps like Bon Appetit, Cocktail Crunch, Supremes and Old Style Crisps come and go – as well as a Smoked Salmon-flavoured crisp. In the early 90s, Tayto launched Ripples (crinkle cut sour cream and onion crisps 'not for the straight and narrow'), and then in 1996 came Ireland's first diet-conscious crisps, LFCs ('Lower Fat Crisps'). In 1999, Scoops and Treble Crunch were also launched for the older crowd. Since the turn of the century, there has been a real proliferation in the more sophisticated snacks for this market – including the tortilla-like Texicanos, Velvet Crunch (made from cassava), Toobz (crisps in a tube) and Lentil Crisps. The upmarket 'Bistro' range has included crunchier, batch-fried – or 'kettle-cooked' – crisps (Crushed Sea Salt and Aged Malt Vinegar, Mature Irish Cheddar Cheese and Spring Onion, Thai Sweet Chilli, Sour Cream and Chive) and gourmet popcorn (Sour Cream and Jalapeño), while the 'Occasions' range has included potato crisps (Mature Cheddar & Spring Onion, Crushed Sea Salt & Aged Malt Vinegar, Amarillo Chilli, Aromatic Sweet Chilli, Rendang Curry), wholegrain chips (Farmhouse Cheese, Sweet Chilli) and snacks (Bacon Fries, Spicy Corn Straws, Four Cheese & Mediterranean Herbs Party Mix). The 'Honest' range has also included popcorn and crisps, and the 2010s also gave us Popcorn Pleasure (microwavable popcorn), Muchos (folded tortilla snacks, inspired by Mexican street food) and Pop Corners (a baked and seasoned tortilla-shaped popcorn chip, launched by popstar Samantha Mumba).

  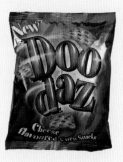 

Some of Tayto's extruded snacks originally made under its 'King' brand in Inchicore.

A newspaper ad from 1973, as Tayto became the distributor for a number of third-party products. Here they had partnered with a Toronto drinks company known primarily for its ginger ale.

In 2006, Tayto collaborated with foul-mouthed puppet brothers Podge and Rodge, launching 'Culchie Crisps' to coincide with the first series of *The Podge and Rodge Show*. According to the packet, Podge had been wondering 'for years what to do with all the spuds growing out of Rodge's ears'. His solution? These 'gloriously thick country crisps that bring out the culchie in everyone'. As well as Buffalo Breath, there was a Cheese & Onion Breath flavour – 'inspired by two-week-old cheesy socks and Rodge's aromatic onion breath'.

The Tayto Chocolate Bar sent fans into a frenzy upon its launch in 2013.

Arguably Tayto's most innovative – and inarguably the most divisive – offering of all was 2013's Tayto Bar, a 'Milk Chocolate Bar with Cheese & Onion Crisps'. This came about by accident, having started life as a normal chocolate bar with Tayto-branded packaging, sold as a souvenir in the Tayto Park gift shop. Legend has it that somebody bought one and posted a photo of it to social media, inadvertently leading others to believe that the bar contained crisps – wishful thinking potentially inspired by the coalesced essence of Coolock in bygone days, and the uniquely Irish predilection for mixing cheese and onion crisps with chocolate.

The ever-observant quick thinkers of Tayto were immediately on the phone to the artisanal chocolatiers of Butlers, who crushed crisps into a bar mould and delivered a prototype within a few days. Butlers had a minimum order quantity of 10,000 bars, which seemed like an optimistic sales target to John O'Connor and his team – but this first batch barely ever made it into the shops before they were all gone. Nationwide pandemonium ensued, and more than a million Tayto bars were sold over the next six months. Butlers employees chalked up some serious overtime as desperate consumers flocked to Facebook groups dedicated to sightings of the bar. According to Charles Coyle of Tayto Park, there were even some devious types buying boxes of them from the gift shop and reselling them online for three times the price – forcing them to introduce a strict limit of two bars per person. Some retailers even held Tayto to ransom, threatening to withdraw their usual order of crisps unless they could be promised some bars alongside their delivery. One Tayto sales rep in a branded van even found himself being pulled over by the Gardaí. Rolling down his window, he feared the worst; perhaps he'd accidentally broken the speed limit? He needn't have worried. 'You wouldn't have any of those chocolate bars, would you?' asked the Bean Garda.

All that said, neither the Tayto Bar nor Fizzy Cola Tayto marked the first time that Tayto produced a concoction that defied the established boundaries of the food pyramid. Behold a 1961 ad for Tayto Cheese & Onion Soup, which didn't cause *quite* as much hype and mass hysteria as the chocolate bar:

The diverse range of Tayto-marketed products in the 70s – from drinks to chocolate bars – echoes Joe's pre-Tayto pursuits with Associated Agencies, when he imported pens, preserves and whatever else he thought there was a niche in the market for. 'When you're in this business', he once explained, 'you get samples from all over the world from people who want me to sell their products in Ireland – but I prefer to make their products in Ireland and then sell them abroad. Isn't that a much better attitude?' Also visible in this shot is Lona, an orange-flavoured drink in a triangular cardboard container. (Arrow Advertising)

THE TAYTO
FANCLUB

Dublin artist Orla Walsh paints iconic brands in a Warhol-inspired pop art style. 'Most of my pop artwork is based on items that I have a connection to in my life', according to Walsh, 'specifically from my childhood in the 1970s.' This colourful journey through Tayto's history proudly hangs in the Tayto Snacks boardroom in Kilbrew.

AN ENDURING LEGACY

Tayto is a rarity in that it is an omnipresent household name in Ireland but not *particularly* well known or readily available overseas. This unique combo means that Tayto is still, in a way, like a local hidden gem, the password to a secret society, and an initiation ceremony for outsiders. Searching for records about Tayto in the Irish newspaper archives, it becomes evident that the brand took on a different role around the early 90s. Although Tayto had long been the national snack, this is when casual references to 'Tayto' in the media seem to have increased exponentially. One could posit that this coincides with a time that the majority of journalists and interviewees were suddenly people who had grown up with Tayto in their lives. Tayto was no longer a recently established company; it was now a heritage brand, a national institution, a key facet of Irishness, an instant nostalgia trigger, and even a byword for anything crunchy and moreish. Since this time, Tayto is nearly guaranteed a mention whenever Irish people abroad are discussed or interviewed, whenever an Irish celebrity is asked about their childhood memories (particularly in relation to summer holidays or school tours), and whenever a food writer wishes to emphasize the appealingly crispy nature of a dish (one dish at a high-end restaurant is 'crisp as a fresh Tayto'; others tend to be 'as crunchy and delicious as Tayto' or 'as fiendish as Tayto').

As Ireland's Celtic Tiger economy started to slow down in 2007, economist David McWilliams suggested that a 'Taytometer' would be a more accurate indication of the number of people emigrating than anything in a government press release – the 'Taytometer' being the total amount of money being spent on Tayto crisps at Dublin Airport. During that past year, around €96,000 worth of Tayto had been bought there, and McWilliams was certain that the Taytometer was about to see a huge increase as the economy bombed and people fled the country clutching a multipack of Cheese & Onion for comfort. Throughout the 2010s, *Checkout Magazine* conducted a number of 'Diaspora Decides' studies into the food most missed by expats abroad. Tayto topped the poll every year but one, raking up as much as 64 per cent of the vote – well ahead of our national teas, chocolate, rashers, sausages, biscuits, bread and butter. To try to put an end to the decades-long tradition of stuffing crisps into suitcases before flights to Australia, Irish businessman Eamon Eastwood set up a company called Taste Ireland from his Sydney bedroom in 2004. After auctioning off a single bag of Cheese & Onion for $25 to one homesick Kilkenny man during a GAA fundraiser in a pub, Eastwood founded Taste with a sole focus on supplying Tayto to Irish pubs. In recent years, they've managed to partner with huge Aussie supermarkets like Coles and Woolworths, resulting in thousands of dedicated 'Irish' sections in stores across the country. With Tayto their best-selling product, it seems like the days of Irish mammies spending a fortune on stamps, and the days of hoovering crisp crumbs out of suitcases, may have finally come to an end.

Irish-American comedian Des Bishop once said that 'It's great that a company like Tayto can create such a connection with the people of Ireland. If I'm gigging abroad and I make a joke about Tayto, every single Irish person in the audience gets it.' In his book *Tickling the English*, comedian Dara Ó Briain tells a story about presenting a black-tie event in the swish Burlington Hotel, after which he was approached by a Tayto representative named Mick. After a friendly chat about Tayto, Mick ran out to his car to fetch Ó Briain a huge box containing forty-eight packets of crisps, which the comedian then had to accessorize with his tuxedo for the remainder of the evening. After telling this story during a recorded live special, an audience member flings a bag of Tayto towards him, which he deftly catches mid-sentence and then happily munches on throughout his encore. Open any Irish newspaper at random and you're likely to see somebody singing the praises of Tayto – from former Taoiseach Leo Varadkar ('My favourite thing about Ireland is our unique culinary delights like red lemonade and Tayto crisps. You won't find anything quite like them anywhere else.') to investigative journalist Donal McIntyre ('If I had to order a last meal, I'd have a giant bag of Tayto and die a happy man.') In his 2014 book, *Eating for Ireland*, foodie Tom Doorley writes that 'The strength of the smell and the flavour of Tayto cheese-and-onion crisps is legendary.'

Pictured around the time of their debut album in 1999, boyband Westlife enjoy a bag of Tayto each. The pop group's first sponsorship deal was a modest arrangement with Tayto, to send off a number of empty packets in exchange for a Westlife beanie hat. One lucky fan also won a trip to London to meet the guys at the 'Smash Hits' awards.

No visit to Ireland is complete without a few packets of Tayto – something that TV chef Nigella Lawson can attest to. Having first tasted Tayto on a visit to Dublin in 2018, she has since taken to social media on several occasions to profess that 'The only cheese and onion crisps I like are the Tayto ones.' Noel and Liam Gallagher of rock group Oasis are another two English superfans, having spent many childhood summers visiting their grandmother in Charlestown, Co. Mayo. During one such visit in 1994, just before the release of their debut album, Noel admitted to an interviewer, 'I didn't really come here to visit my granny. It's actually a lie. I came here to fuel my addiction to Brunches, Silvermints, Carrolls, Major and Tayto Crisps.' The fame, glory and riches that followed did little to change Noel's tastes. Fifteen years later, just before playing to 80,000 fans in Meath, he posted on his blog, 'Slane Castle tomorrow. Silvermints, Tayto Crisps and Brunches! YUMMY.' In fact, it seems that Tayto might be the one thing that the famously combative Gallagher brothers can agree on. In 2019, Liam tweeted that 'Taytos are the best crisps in the universe' and then, during an interview with Ian Dempsey, said, 'I got given a box of

Taytos, so they got their little special seat on the plane. I love them crisps, man. They're like crack. I've gone through about twenty packets. I need to get rid of them. I need to give them to someone else. I can't be walloping boxes of Taytos before gigs, man.'

'What a belter' – Liam Gallagher, after one of his visits, ensuring that his precious cargo is kept safe on the flight back to England.

No discussion of music and Tayto would be complete without mentioning a song by Pat Quinn of Inis Oírr, 'The Great Potato Feud,' which depicts a drunken argument about the best variety of potato, and contains the immortal – yet perhaps controversial – line 'Just because you work for Tayto doesn't mean you know potatoes.' And nothing establishes that a story is set in Ireland as immediately as the appearance of a packet of Tayto, which is why they tend to pop up regularly in books, movies, TV shows – and even plays like *Disco Pigs* by Enda Walsh and *The Lonesome West* by Academy Award winner Martin McDonagh. In the latter, 'fecking Taytos' form a key part of the action, inciting a number of passionate arguments and even physical fights between three brothers. In Roddy Doyle's play *No Messin' with the Monkeys,* we meet a family of monkeys that sneak out of Dublin Zoo after dark to – amongst other things – work night shifts at the Tayto factory in Coolock. Tayto also appears in the 'Aisling' series of novels by Emer McLysaght and Sarah Breen, as well as in books by Eoin Colfer, Amy Huberman, Marian Keyes, John Boyne, Ross O'Carroll Kelly and dozens of other novels and memoirs.

The 1992 Irish classic *Into the West* follows Ballymun brothers Tito and Ossie on a mythical horseback quest. However, the majority of Irish people – as well as dozens of reviews from the time – tend to refer to the older brother as 'Tayto'. Despite not actually being his name, it's as though an entire nation of singleminded crisp connoisseurs decided that it was, eager to see subliminal Tayto advertising even where there was none. Probably the most curious *actual* representation of Tayto on the silver screen is in Henry Selick's film adaptation of *James and the Giant Peach*. Near the beginning of the movie, James – a deprived and starved orphan – rummages around in the kitchen bin, looking for something to eat. He finds a large, empty bag of Tayto which he brings to his bedroom to lick clean. Turning the bag inside out, a singing James uses the greaseproof paper as the canvas for a crayon drawing of New York City – which he turns into a lantern and sends off into the night sky, setting in stop-motion his magical journey to the city. There are two interesting anachronisms here: not only does the story begin in England – where Tayto has never been readily available – but it is set in 1949, back when Spud Murphy was still selling pens and other imported goods from his Nassau Street office. One can only assume that an overzealous, homesick Irish prop master was responsible for this glorious tribute. A more period correct usage of Tayto can be spotted in the 2023 action film *In the Land of Saints and Sinners*, starring Liam Neeson – where a mass of 1970s Tayto packets populate the background of the movie, set in Troubles-era Donegal.

When *Desperate Housewives* star Eva Longoria visited Dublin in 2014, she took to Twitter to ask her fans for tourist tips. 'They gave me restaurant recommendations and historic places,' she later told chat show host Seth Meyers, 'and they say you can't be in Dublin without eating a Tayto crisp!'

After filming a brief cameo for *Star Wars: The Force Awakens* on Skellig Michael, actor Mark Hamill returned to Ireland in 2016 to star in the sequel *The Last Jedi*. After shooting wrapped, he posted this photograph online, with the caption 'How I will miss IRELAND! Its beauty, its people, its... snack food.' A couple of days later, he tried to restore balance by tweeting that he hadn't meant to 'endorse a product or do an inadvertent advert.' Little did he know the power – or indeed force – of Tayto.

TAYTO
FOR AUNTIE PAT

Fourpence

Pinch the greaseproof bag
and pull
to release a puff of luxury
rich savory-roasted
cheese and onion
potatoe wafers
the salt in a tiny sachet
invented off fruity Moore Street
where Joe Murphy
the Lord be good to him
was washing spuds in a bath

And here's to Tayto Murphy
who toasted the devil one night
he lifted his glass to irony
and drank to his heart's delight
may the hell-fires heat his ovens
and sinners queue to buy
the roasted pinks they harvested
from the clay in hell's black sky

His fourpence worth of Heaven
Joe Murphy's gift of life
the finely sliced potatoe
his magic eye his wife

Irish urchins reared on prayers
and disrespectful rhymes
respect with their fourpenny offerings
and millions of fourpenny times
gone their hunger gone the cold
a famine turned to feast
Joe Murphy's scruffy angels toast
their cheese and onion priest

BY ANON

TAYTO CRISPS
FOR DUNSTAN AND MORGAN

When I open the package of Tayto Crisps
they're all there, happy as a commercial,
full of snap and taste.

And I do taste them, I taste one or two quite deliberately.
Smokey Bacon, Salt and Vinegar or Cheese and Onion,
I savor them all, fully aware of their goodness,
such a welcome my mouth has for them.

Then I shake out a small handful, I don't want to spill them.
Then another then another and then another.
I am surprised at how many there are.
I eat more quickly, my molars are crammed with them,
the bag will never be emptied.

Then, before you know it, the bag is empty.
There are only fragments left, and grains of salt.
I must put my tongue to work now like a toothpick.
I must lick my fingers.

BY KNUTE SKINNER

The rich history and richer flavour of Tayto has even
inspired poets down through the years, as seen
here in 'Tayto' (author unknown) and 'Tayto Crisps'
(1984), by Clare – via Missouri – poet Knute Skinner.

EPILOGUE: TAYTO TODAY

And that, dear crisp-loving reader, is how Tayto came into being and grew from a tiny cottage industry into a national institution and cultural phenomenon, in record time.

The ever-youthful Joe Murphy lived his life adhereing to his personal motto, 'Show me, don't tell me' – a philosophy that helped him on his way to becoming Ireland's 'Potato Crisp King', as he was often referred to in the media. Having made a packet and then handed over the reins of Tayto, Joe moved with Bunny to the Hotel del Golf in Las Brisas, where he lived out his days boating, golfing, reading, writing and travelling the world. Despite playing golf almost every day, he wasn't a particularly talented player. 'His swing was like the mark of Zorro,' according to his son Stephen. On the one occasion that he hit a hole-in-one, he threw himself the party to end all parties. After he passed away, just a couple of weeks after 9/11, his ashes were scattered at sea, as Rudyard Kipling's *If—* was recited from the deck. Then, to the sound of Frank Sinatra's 'My Way', mourners threw handfuls of Tayto Cheese & Onion overboard to float alongside his remains (a uniquely poetic take on the tradition of throwing soil on top of a coffin).

Joe's eldest son, Joe Jr, moved to Toronto in 1972, where he built up his own snack empire before passing away in 2018. Bunny died in Spain the following year, and Spud is survived by his four remaining children, Yvonne, Barry, Peter and Stephen.

In 1956, two years after starting at Tayto, Seamus Burke married and settled in Glasnevin with his wife, Bridget. A keen gardener, fisher and home movie maker, he worked for Tayto until his retirement in January 1983. Tragically, he suffered a stroke and died less than two months later, on the 20th of March, at the age of sixty-four. In 2021, a blue plaque was unveiled on the site of his childhood home in Cloonacool, commemorating his contribution to crisp history.

After Raymond Coyle stepped away from Tayto, he turned his focus to his theme park and other investments – including SyncerChi kombucha (incidentally founded by Laura Murphy, granddaughter of Joe) and Irish Cone and Wafer (who had once, many years prior, supplied Joe with the wafers that went into his 'Peanut Whip'). Ray passed away in 2022, at the age of sixty-nine. At his funeral mass in Curragha, the priest praised his 'strong personality', 'gifts and talents and visions' and 'sense of humour that caught many an unsuspecting victim unaware' – one such gag being his elaborate explanation as to how they get the buffalo into Buffalo crisps (despite the fact that they're actually vegetarian friendly!) Emerald Park stayed in the family, and is now run by Ray's son Charles.

Today, Tayto Snacks employs around 400 people at its 80,000 square foot factory in Kilbrew, and processes around 10 per cent of the nation's annual potato crop. In recent years, it has established a Care in the Community Committee, partnered with Food Cloud, and developed a 'Potato Pals' programme for primary school students.

Due to phenomenal demand, the humble Tayto crisp sandwich – a true Irish national delicacy – was given its very own pop-up shop on Wicklow Street in Dublin in 2015. (Sean McDonagh)

There's nothing as rare as an Irish family album without a Tayto cameo. (**LEFT**) Tayto loving sisters Elaine and Sinead Smith enjoying a snack at the Killygarry GAA grounds in County Cavan, in 1994. (**ABOVE**) The five siblings of baby Catherine Keane Murphy munch away during a family photo taken in 1977.

In keeping with the company's tradition of sponsorship, Tayto has sponsored the Comórtas Peile Páidi Ó Sé and donated funds to Olympian athletes (including boxer Katie Taylor and Ray Coyle's Olympian daughter, Natalya), while Tayto Park has served as the main sponsor of the Meath GAA teams. Tayto has also sponsored the Christmas pantomime in the Gaiety Theatre, which once featured Mr Tayto taking to the stage alongside Cinderella, to fling packets of crisps into a baying crowd. Mr Tayto has even become a shop-keeper, setting up a crisp sandwich stall – with all proceeds going to charity – and opening pop-up merchandise shops in Dublin city and Dublin Airport.

In 2024, Tayto celebrated seventy years of crisp-making. Mr Tayto got his own float in Dublin's St Patrick's Day parade, six-ty-eight years after the company had sent along six branded vans to make its mark. It also launched 'Tay70' commemorative packaging, an interactive nationwide roadshow, seventy days of competitions and a postmark on all mail franked by An Post ... not to mention a certain book, telling the story in full for the first time ever.

The Tayto Snacks team 2024. (Simon McDermott, Leinster Photos)

Like any company so successful that it outlives its founder, Tayto has gone through many iterations as different caretakers have been tasked with overseeing its continuing journey and evolution. Over the years, the brand has changed hands several times, and each parent company has told and sold *their* own version of the Tayto legend. But at the centre of *this* story, and despite huge market shifts, changing tastes and diet fads, Tayto Cheese & Onion remains the most popular crisp in Ireland – and Mr Tayto one of the most recognizable and beloved public figures in the country, to the point that *Irish Times* journalist Patrick Freyne included him on his list of '30 Real Irish Icons'.

Tayto is indeed more than just ... more than just a crisp. The sight, feel, scent, sound and flavour evoked by a packet of Cheese & Onion has the remarkable ability to overwhelm the senses and instantly transport any Irish person to some of the most memorable times of their lives. But Tayto is also more than just a nostalgia trip, a business success story, the Hiberno-English word for 'crisps', a distinctly Irish curiosity or a bottomless well of national pride. Tayto is all of these things, and more. So isn't it funny to think that it all started with a Liberties man complaining about some stale crisps in Swords, before letting his curiosity run wild? 'Just something to think about', as a time traveller in a Tayto ad once said, 'next time you get caught eating a packet of Tayto in the back of history class.'